Manson & Woods Christie

Catalogue of the Marlborough gems

Being a collection of works in cameo and intaglio

Manson & Woods Christie

Catalogue of the Marlborough gems
Being a collection of works in cameo and intaglio

ISBN/EAN: 9783741129780

Manufactured in Europe, USA, Canada, Australia, Japa

Cover: Foto ©Thomas Meinert / pixelio.de

Manufactured and distributed by brebook publishing software
(www.brebook.com)

Manson & Woods Christie

Catalogue of the Marlborough gems

CATALOGUE

OF

THE MARLBOROUGH GEMS,

BEING A COLLECTION OF

Works in Cameo and Intaglio,

FORMED BY

GEORGE, 3rd DUKE OF MARLBOROUGH,

PURCHASED BY THE LATE

DAVID BROMILOW, ESQ.,

Of Bitteswell Hall, Lutterworth,

THE PROPERTY OF MRS. JARY:

WHICH

Will be Sold by Auction by

Messrs. CHRISTIE, MANSON & WOODS,

AT THEIR GREAT ROOMS,

8 KING STREET, ST. JAMES'S SQUARE,

On MONDAY, JUNE 26, 1899,

And Three Following Days,

AT ONE O'CLOCK PRECISELY.

————◦◦◦◦◦◦————

May be viewed Wednesday, Thursday and Friday preceding, and Catalogues (CATALOGUES, WITH FOURTEEN ILLUSTRATIONS, PRICE ONE GUINEA) had, at Messrs. CHRISTIE, MANSON and WOODS' Offices, 8 *King Street, St. James's Square, S.W.*

CONDITIONS OF SALE.

———o———

I. THE highest Bidder to be the Buyer; and if any dispute arise between two or more Bidders, the Lot so in dispute shall be immediately put up again and re-sold.

II. No person to advance less than 1*s.*; above Five Pounds, 5*s.*; and so on in proportion.

III. In the case of Lots upon which there is a reserve, the Auctioneer shall have the right to bid on behalf of the seller.

IV. The Purchasers to give in their Names and Places of Abode, and to pay down 5*s.* in the Pound, or more, in part of payment, or the whole of the Purchase-Money, *if required*; in default of which, the Lot or Lots so purchased to be immediately put up again and re-sold.

V. The lots to be taken away and paid for, whether genuine and authentic or not, with all faults and errors of description, at the Buyer's expense and risk, within Two days from the Sale; Messrs. CHRISTIE, MANSON and WOODS not being responsible for the correct description, genuineness, or authenticity of, or any fault or defect in, any Lot; and making no warranty whatever.

VI. To prevent inaccuracy in delivery, and inconvenience in the settlement of the Purchases, no Lot can on any account be removed during the time of Sale; and the remainder of the Purchase-Money must absolutely be paid on the delivery.

VII. Upon failure of complying with the above Conditions, the Money deposited in part of payment shall be forfeited; all Lots uncleared within the time aforesaid shall be re-sold by public or private Sale, and the deficiency (if any) attending such re-sale shall be made good by the Defaulter at this Sale.

INTRODUCTION.

N.B.—The following is abridged from the Catalogue and Introduction by M. H. Nevil Story-Maskelyne, M.A., F.R.S.

THE collection of cameos and intaglios of which this is a Catalogue, has for nearly a century deservedly possessed a wide reputation. The two splendid volumes printed and distributed by the third Duke of Marlborough in 1780 and 1791, wherein a hundred of the most remarkable pieces in his collection were described and figured, would alone have sufficed to establish this fame for the " Marlborough Gems." To the archæologist, however, the cabinet at Blenheim has always possessed an additional and a singular interest, from its including the collection of gems that had been formed by that famous Earl of Arundel who, during the troubled times of the first Charles, found a solace for the abridgment of his dignities in collecting works of art and monuments of antiquity.

The Arundel Gems, however, formed only one part of the great collection of works in cameo and intaglio brought together by George, third Duke of Marlborough ; nor were gems the only, though probably they were the favourite, objects that he collected.

Among the pictures at Blenheim there is one famous canvas on which Sir Joshua Reynolds has handed down to us the portrait of the third Duke, his Duchess, and their elder children. In his hand his Grace holds a large cameo, and at his side stands his son the Marquis of Blandford, carrying under his arm a red morocco case ; one of the ten similar cases that still contain the collection of gems. This gem-case serves at once to introduce a mass of effective colour into the picture, and to complete the motive of the scene by presenting to us the Duke in his character of a gem collector.

The particular cameo he holds is that numbered 390 in this Catalogue ; it was one of the gems collected individually by the Duke's excellent taste, and it no doubt claimed on that account, no less than from its high intrinsic importance, a place of honour among his gems.

The proportion which the part of the Collection thus formed by the Duke, by separate purchases in Italy and at home, bears to the whole of the Cabinet, amounts to about the half.

The remaining half is composed of two distinct collections united by the Duke to his own, each of which was important and celebrated.

The one has already been alluded to as formed, in the early half of the century previous to that in which the Duke was a collector, by the illustrious Thomas Howard, Earl of Arundel, the Mæcenas of the Caroline period ; the other was brought together by William, second Earl of Bessborough and third

A 2

Viscount Duncannon, a nobleman some thirty years senior to the third Duke, who had no doubt cultivated his taste, and in part formed his collection of gems during a period of travel on the Continent, which terminated in 1739, the same year in which the third Duke of Marlborough was born.

Of the two collections which thus became blended with the third Duke's acquisitions, to shine with united lustre as " the Marlborough Gems," the first to demand a notice is that formed by Lord Arundel. Alike from the character of its contents and from its authentic pedigree, the Arundelian Collection stands now almost alone in interest. One has only to consider how very few of the existing gem collections in Europe were in being before the beginning of the last century, and what confusion was introduced into the study of gems as records of the past, by the forgeries and fabrications carried on chiefly in Italy during that century, in order to recognise the value that must needs attach to a collection formed at the date when a Stuart sovereign held in abeyance the ducal rank of the proud and accomplished head of the house of Howard. In the midst of such a collection we stand so far at least on solid ground, that we may feel sure of every gem with a classical subject that we examine belonging either to the ages of Greek or Roman art, or to that long-after age in which the classical arts were revived and seemed to burst forth into a sort of preternatural rejuvenescence. But the gem-engraver of the Revival never or seldom copied slavishly the works of antiquity ; he aspired to convey their sentiment, but with a freedom of treatment to which, in fact, whatever was noble in the Renaissance school was due. He perfected his technical methods, and in this respect could challenge the finest works of Roman artists. That his hand never acquired the subtle and spontaneous cunning, or his spirit the simply grand conception of the Greek masters, is only to say that as " Greece was living Greece no more," so, too, the myths of that once living Greece were dead. The comparison of the gems of the Cinque-cento or Renaissance school, is therefore rather to be made with those that were called into existence during the Roman Revival of art, under Hadrian and the Antonines, than with the gems of the ages when Greek art flourished on its own soil, or had been freshly imported into Imperial Rome.

It is more particularly with the gems of the latter class that, the works of the last century sought to compete, and sought too often to compete, not in freedom of design and its attendent freedom of treatment, but by simply bringing an improved and in fact almost perfect technical method to bear in multiplying copies of antique originals.

From such gems as these, then, the Arundelian cases were entirely free.

The gems—and we may presume the whole of them—were included in the portion of Lord Arundel's property that descended to his son and successor, Henry Frederick Lord Maltravers, and from him they passed to the sixth Duke of Norfolk, his son—the Duke to whom Oxford is indebted for one portion of the Arundelian Marbles. His son, the seventh Duke, succeeded to the possession of them ; but now, by a strange fate, they passed away from the House of Howard : for the Arundelian antiquities, including the gems, were retained . as her property by the divorced Duchess, that Lady Mary

Mordaunt who, in 1705, five years after the decree for her divorce was passed in the House of Lords, died and bequeathed the whole of her estate to her husband, Sir John Germain. She had previously sold the other antiquities; but the gems passed to Sir John under her will.

In 1718, Sir John married for his second wife the Lady Elizabeth Berkeley, daughter of Charles, second Earl of Berkeley, and by his will he left that lady in possession of all his property.

Thus the Arundelian Cabinet of Gems passed by a second step of alienation from Arundel Castle into the possession of Sir John's widow, the Lady Elizabeth Germain. There seems no reason to suppose that during these changes of ownership the collection had been despoiled of any of its treasures; so that we may fairly presume that Lady Elizabeth possessed it much in the state in which it was left by the noble connoisseur who formed it. And, fortunately, we have a valuable and trustworthy record of the contents of the collection at this time in a catalogue, a copy of which, in manuscript, dated 1727, exists in the library of the Society of Antiquaries. The "Lady Betty" survived till 1769; but in October 1762, her great niece, the Lady Mary Beauclerk, was married to Lord Charles Spencer, brother of the third Duke of Marlborough. This lady was the daughter of Lord Vere Beauclerk, created Lord Vere of Hanworth, who subsequently became fourth Duke of St. Albans, and whose wife was Mary Chambers, daughter and heiress of Thomas Chambers, Esq., of Hanworth, and Lady Mary his wife, sister to Lady Elizabeth Germain.

From her great aunt Lady Elizabeth, the Lady Mary Beauclerk, the bride of 1762, received the gems—a splendid gift. Perhaps gems were looked on as a sort of bridal appanage descending as a casket of family jewels might have descended in each successive generation to the lady through whose alliance a family hoped to be perpetuated: such, at least, seems to have been the case with the bequest of the Hunsdon gems at Berkeley Castle in 1603.

By a family arrangement, however, the Arundelian Collection now passed from the hands of Lady Mary Spencer to add to the magnificence, and embellish with a fresh archæological value, the collection which the Duke, her brother-in-law, was at that time busy in forming. And it has now, after its various alienations of ownership, passed into a haven of rest, in which, for above a century, it has lain undisturbed. Once, indeed, some seven years before the gems had reached this final destination, they had been offered by Lady Elizabeth to the trustees of the then nascent British Museum for the great sum of 10,000l. The offer was not accepted. This sum, however, if the collection was still entire, must have been much below what it originally cost; for the Earl of Arundel is declared by Evelyn to have given that very sum for a collection of gems that he purchased of Daniel Nys, of Venice; and Evelyn himself was employed by the Earl in collecting such objects in Rome and other parts of Italy.

On examining the Arundelian Collection, one is struck with the singular little gem engraved on ruby or ruby spinel—the crowned portrait of Charles cinq, king of France, No. 583 of this Catalogue, which is most remarkable;

as its date must have been early in the second half of the 14th century.*
Among the important intaglios of the Arundelian Cabinet, we may instance a
famous gem (No. 341), the Rape of the Palladium from the Trojan Temple :—

Impius ex quo
Tydides sed enim. scelerumque inventor Ulysses,
Fatale adgressi sacrato avellere templo
Palladium, cæsis summæ custodibus arcis,
Corripuere sacrom effigiem,

The Medusa on a sapphire (No. 98); the marvellously fine intaglio portrait
(No. 122) of Marcia, or some lady of an earlier time, on a sardine, as
remarkable for its magnitude as for its fine execution, in a style that we can
scarcely attribute to the artists of the Renaissance; the beautifully designed
little Bacchus on a beryl (No. 183); the noble intaglio bust of Mars (No. 109);
the fine cameo representing Ariadne (No. 194), may be cited among the more
exquisite of the antique works that had a place with the Arundelian Gems.

The MS. catalogue of the Arundelian Gems that has been alluded to as
existing in the ; library of the Society of Antiquaries (No. 43, Smart
Lethieullier), is a copy from an original catalogue "lent by the Right
Honourable the Lady Betty Jermain, owner of the cabinet." That original,
no doubt, passed with the gems into the possession of the Duke of Marlborough; and on it, and on Natter's catalogue of the Bessborough gems, his
Grace founded a catalogue, which, besides giving an account of the Arundel
and Bessborough collections, was to embrace the descriptions of the gems of
his own private collection. But this catalogue, which was to have been
printed, seems never to have been completed. Copies in manuscript, in
various stages of progress, remain, and in some of these the original descriptions of the Arundel catalogue are simply copied, the Italian addenda to the
latter being converted into Latin.

The title of the MS. at Somerset House is as follows :—

Gemmæ incisæ excisæque, maximâ ex parte antiquæ, quas cœlatura
insignes, auroque ornatas ingens copia, multiplex color, magnitudo lapidum
sculptorum mirabilis et prorsus inimitabilis ars summopere commēdant.

Thesaurus olim Arundellianus primis Europæ cimeliis sane invidendus
qui nunc in Ædibus nobilis Matronæ Dⁿᵃ Elizabethæ Germain, Londini
summâ curâ servatur.

The Catalogue from which this is a transcript was, however, itself a copy,
made by some Italian hand; probably not far from the date of the transcript,
1727; and to this copyist certain Italian notices, completing the descriptions,
were due. The allusion to Stosch's work at the end of the description of the

* That gems were engraved at so early a date is proved by an observation of
Mr. King's, to whom I am indebted for the light thrown on the date of this gem,
while this work is passing through the press. Mr. King observes, in confirma-
tion of this ruby being the actual signet of Charles, how Ammonato, in his
'History of Florence' (p. 741), mentions that Peruzzi, the Florentine singolare
intagliatore di pietre, forged the seal of Durazzo in the year 1379.

gem (Thec. E. No. 2), the Rape of the Palladium (No. 341 of this Catalogue), and also in the account of the cameo No. 160, is sufficient to show that the Italian annotator did not write till after 1724.

The more remote original was undoubtedly a true Arundelian Catalogue, describing the gems as they originally stood in the cabinet of Lord Arundel. Indeed, a note at the end of the MS. at Somerset House records it to have been : " Estratto del antico catalogo delle Gemme intagliate, e scolpite, che furono gia il trosoro piu riguardévole del famosissimo Museo Arondelliano, le quali quasi tutte legate in oro, che monta al valore di piu che quatro centocinquanta doppie. Sono conservate in cinque casette notate con le lettere A, B, C, D, E, con un ragguaglio piu distinto et esatto delle differenza accidentáli di quelle."

The Catalogue contains the description of 263 gems, arranged in the five cases ; 133 being intaglios, and 130 cameos. The descriptions are in Latin; an Italian addition, already alluded to, descriptive of the stone, and often also of the setting, being appended to the account of each gem.

The gems brought together by Lord Bessborough at the time the Duke of Marlborough acquired them, had grown into a collection of some importance, not only in consequence of the judicious selections by which they had been increased, but notably by two considerable purchases. By one of these his Lordship added to his Cabinet forty-five gems, the property of Philip Dormer, fourth Earl of Stanhope ; and by the other purchase, on the occasion of the sale by auction of the collection of Medina, a Jew, at Leghorn, he acquired forty-seven more ; and some of these must have been amongst the choicest in the Medina Cabinet. The selection made from that collection by or on behalf of Lord Bessborough, comprised several admirable and authentic pieces. Among these may be instanced the interesting but mutilated statuette representing Marciana in Apotheosis (No. 457) ; and to this part of the collection of Lord Bessborough belonged the gem (No. 316) once held worthy of passing as a gift from an emperor to a pope. Here also is seen the beautiful Muse in bust (No. 70).

Among the gems acquired from Lord Chesterfield was the famous intaglio (No. 270), the dog star Sirius, deeply cut into a splendid garnet, and taking the highest rank for its execution and finish among the gems of any age. The taste of this accomplished nobleman is also well illustrated in the interesting portraits that adorned his small cabinet ; such as the fine little intaglio representing Marcus Junius Brutus (No. 375), of which No. 376 is probably a copy by Natter's hand ; the Sabina (No. 454) ; the Antoninus Pius (No. 462) ; and the head of Caracalla (No. 485), engraved on a fine sapphire, and interesting as showing the mastery of the engraver at that period over so stubborn a material ; nor should the beautiful little ring (No. 551) be omitted as an exquisite example among many of the goldsmith's art.

The acquisition of these two important additions nearly doubled the number of gems that composed Lord Bessborough's Cabinet. Including them, it now numbered two hundred pieces, and was catalogued in French by

Laurent Natter, the famous gem engraver, and published in the year 1761. The gems, as described in Natter's Catalogue, have, with the exception of four, been identified, and references are given to his descriptions under the different gems in this Catalogue. Without doubt his Lordship had been helped in his acquisitions by the use of Natter's professional opportunities, and had been guided in his selections by the great engraver's excellent taste and intimate acquaintance with the technical details of his art.

As evidencing the high character and value of many of the gems collected by Lord Bessborough himself, we may instance the great Medusa phalera (No. 100), one of the grandest works on such a hard material as chalcedony in the world; or the deeply cut bust of Pallas (No. 81), on amethyst. The noble intaglio of Jupiter Serapis (No. 5), cut in a large amethyst pebble; the vast Nicolo (No. 256), with its strange African engraving; the Apollo mourning Coronis (No. 60); the athlete (No. 621); these, too, are illustrations of the skill and judgment with which the Earl of Bessborough—or rather, perhaps, we should say the Viscount Duncannon, for it was under this his title of courtesy, through his earlier manhood that he was best known to the gem amateur—was guided in his selections for his cabinet.

If we abstract from the Blenheim Collection as it now stands the gems of the Arundelian and Bessborough Cabinets, we shall find remaining a still noble collection of gems, amounting in number to about the half, and enriched by many splendid pieces, as remarkable in material as they are beautiful or interesting as works of art. This is the portion of the Blenheim Collection that was formed by the third Duke. Foremost among these gems stands the great sardonyx (No. 482); one which will ever rank as one of the most important cameos known, as well on account of the magnitude as of the beautiful character and even deposit of the layers of sard that form the stone.

Then, also, the Augustus already alluded to (No. 390) is a cameo of rare interest and beauty.

Among the intaglios in his Grace's Collection notice may in particular be drawn to the following: the Hermes (No. 165), a noble Greek work;[*] the Holderness Hermes (No. 167), which with its inscription of the name ΔΙΟCΚΟΥΙΔΟΥ, has an irreproachable pedigree; the extraordinary but puzzling gem, the green jasper Isis (No. 46); the famous Hercules, with the name ΑΔΜѠΝ (No. 296); the exquisite fragment of Augustus, in the character of Hermes (No. 387); and the Julia of ΝΙΚΑΝΔΡΟΣ, on a tran-

---

[*] It is a very remarkable circumstance that this noble gem was not among the "century" of gems selected by the third Duke for illustration in his work. Worlidge figured it as an Apollo! but Raspe correctly describes the design while he calls the stone a "beryll," with a "bezle" (No. 2375). He also describes two copies, one on "beryll," and one on "cornelian," by Burch senior, both in the Duke's Collection. Raspe implies by "beryll" a fine sard; but probably he has been in error as to the latter "beryll," which must be the amethyst No. 166 in this Collection. The cornelian copy may be that figured by Spilsbury (1781-85) as a gem belonging to the Hon. C. Greville, to whom the Duke may have parted with it, as it is not now among the gems of the Collection.

scendent sard (No. 447). These are beautiful specimens of the antique engravers' work.

It would be difficult now to trace the history of many of the gems collected by the third Duke, or even to find through what channels he obtained them. In the acquisition of many of the pictures at Blenheim he was aided by Mr. John Udney, for whom the influence of the Duke with Lord Halifax procured the appointment to the British Consulship at Venice, about the year 1761. Through him, also, he was in communication with Count Zanetti and other Italians, who profited by the contemporary fashion of gem collecting. It was in this way that the Duke acquired for 600*l.* four gems, the Sabina (No. 455), the Antinous (No. 501), the so-called " Phocion " (No. 538), and the Horatius Cocles (No. 596). With Marchant, some twenty years later, he was in correspondence, sometimes for the purchase of works by Marchant's own hand, sometimes for the acquisition of gems through his agency. This admirable artist appears, so far as can be judged by two or three of his letters, to have been a person of character and of discrimination ; and through him his Grace seems to have acquired the beautiful fragment of the large intaglio of Augustus as Mercury (No. 387), a gem with enough of the Greek touch in its treatment to justify at once Marchant's description of it as a Greek work of importance from its magnitude, and the price paid for it, 23 guineas, a sum contrasting favourably with those paid to Zanetti.

The following gems belonged to one collection, but of the name of the owner and the date of its purchase no record remains. The Isis and Horus (No. 45), bought for 10 guineas ; the Medusa (No. 99), for 40 guineas ; Bacchante's Head (probably that numbered 197), for 70 guineas ; the Horatii (No. 609), for 30 guineas ; and the fine cameo of a Lion seizing a Bull (No. 716), for 50 guineas. These prices are interesting as examples of the sums paid towards the end of the last century for gems.

From another collection, apparently the property of a French gentleman, the Duke selected the following :—The Isis on garnet (No. 44) ; the Venus (No. 135) ; the little cameo (No. 159), with its exquisite mounting, which is a marvel of the jeweller's work of the rarest and most delicate kind : Mercury carrying the Infant Bacchus (No. 169) ; two gems representing Hercules (No. 295 and No. 300) ; the portrait of Mary Queen of Scots (No. 589) ; the Discobolus (No. 623) ; the Elephant trampling a Fish (No. 705) ; and the Lion's Head in cat's-eye (No. 717). The sources of a few other gems purchased by the Duke are noticed under their several descriptions ; and if documents at Blenheim are silent as to the channels through which his Grace procured some three hundred of the gems in his collection, the purchases above recorded will suffice to prove that he had agents and correspondents in many of the important centres of European commerce and luxury.

It is to the centuries between the reign of Augustus and the end of the Antonine period, that we have to refer the major part of the gems in this as in most other fairly selected collections of gems. And among these the gems are most numerous and conspicuous that were worked about the period of the reign of Hadrian, during the marked revival in that reign of the arts that had receded so far in the previous reigns from the perfection of the Augustan age.

To this time belongs of course that marvellously fine Antinous on a black sard, that has been so often copied in the last century (No. 500 in this Catalogue) ; and'to this age, too, must be referred several of the polychrome cameos cut in the differently coloured layers of sardonyx in that reign coming into vogue, the material of which was, perhaps, then supplied in larger and choicer specimens by the extending commerce with the East. Possibly to this age is to be assigned that marvel of art, the great chalcedony phalera (No. 100), though it is difficult to believe that it is not a work of an earlier and a nobler period in the history of art.

Of the classes of gems, Egyptian in their subjects, but belonging in date to the Ptolemaic and Romano-Egyptian periods, there are a few examples in the Blenheim Collection. The portrait (No. 364) of Demetrius Philopator, though not Egyptian, is of Ptolemaic date and Greek workmanship ; and probably the splendid cameo (No. 366) of an Egyptian queen, may claim Greco-Ptolemaic date and origin. So, too, may the cameo on lapis lazuli (No. 319) of two profile busts, probably royal, as Hercules and Iole. The beautiful hyacinthine garnet, with a head of Isis (No. 43), is Romano-Egyptian, if it be not even Ptolemaic ; while the gems, Nos. 44 and 46, belong to the later of these periods. The heads of Serapis, so common under the Roman Empire, were certainly engraved in other parts of the Empire besides Egypt. Of the Mithraic subjects, which the infiltration of the Persian religious system into the Empire had called into existence, there are two examples, described in page 50. Of the works of the Lower Empire after Severus Alexander, a period when gem engraving in Rome had become well-nigh barbarous, we should not expect to find examples in this Collection. Indeed there are not, perhaps, half a dozen Roman gems in it of later date than the reign of Elagabalus, even if we include some of the memorial rings and souvenirs described on page 106 of this Catalogue. Nor, again, of the very numerous gems remaining to our time from the days of the Persian Empire under the Sassanian sovereigns—so conspicuous for the exquisite stones on which their designs are engraved, and for the coarse wheel-wrought character of the designs themselves—were any considered worthy of a place in the Blenheim Collection ; probably, indeed, its noble collector was not acquainted with them at all. Even Byzantine gems are unrepresented in it. These gems are absent, no doubt, for the reason that the art was ceasing to be "classical," as well in subjects as in treatment.

But after the long sleep of the gem-engraver's, as of other classical forms of Art, through those active centuries that we call the Dark Ages, while the civilisation and politics of modern Europe were fermenting out from the great turmoil that attended, and partly caused, the decadence of the divided Empire, came that age of the Renaissance, the era of the Medicis.

Of the re-awakened arts of that era gem engraving was one, and it of course reflected the characters of the rest. Without entering on the history of its growth and progress, we may point to a few of the finer examples of the period in the great Collection under our review. The spinel or ruby signet of Charles cinq of France (No. 588), and the exquisite and famous cameo, the Nuptials of Cupid and Psyche, have already been alluded to when speaking of the Arundel Collection. The latter illustrates by the charm of its drawing, the perfection of its execution, and the relation which the design bears to the form and size of the surface it adorns, all the characteristics of the best time of the Renaissance.

Among the many cameos and portraits of that period, none can surpass the grand head (No. 538), probably representing some personage contemporary with the famous artist Alessandro il Greco who engraved it. The portraiture of that period of art is further represented in the cameo likenesses of the Emperor Charles V., of Philip II. (probably by Jacopo de Trezzo), of Henri IV., and of Cardinal Mazarin.

Among the modern gems, which are especially numerous in the portion of the collection formed by the third Duke himself, are to be found works by Sirletti (the Laocoon, on amethyst, No. 349, is one), by Natter, by Pichler, by Burch, and by Marchant, who aided his Grace in the purchase of some of his finest and most authentically antique gems while resident in Rome.

This sketch would be incomplete without some notice of the materials to the durability of which we owe the preservation, and to the beauty of which is due so much of the charm of a collection of gems. The stones employed by the gem-engraver in ancient times differ but little from those in use for the purpose in the Renaissance and modern ages. The commonest material in each age has been chalcedony in one or other of its numerous and varied forms. Next to chalcedony come the garnets, the amethyst, lapis lazuli, the beryl, the sapphire, the peridot, the emerald ; while some late gems, chiefly amulets, engraved with gnostic and astrological subjects, are met with on hæmatite and occasionally on magnetite, the mineral forms of two of the oxides of iron. With the exception of the last two, these stones engraved with antique work occur with a frequency represented by the order in which we have recounted them.

But the chalcedonic minerals offer the most coveted materials to the gem-engraver, who prizes their fine grain—or rather absence of grain and crystalline cleavage—their toughness, and their hardness, which is such as to yield most readily to the materials (diamond and emery dust) wherewith he charges his wheel ; while on the other hand they are able to resist the abrasion of ordinary materials, and the more subtle erosion of Time. These stones also are all susceptible of an excellent polish, and are many of them endowed with the gift of beautiful colour. Hence to one stone of any other material we find perhaps ten composed of some form of chalcedony. Chalcedony is composed of silica in a form devoid of visible crystallisation, whilst quartz is that earth completely crystallised. The amethyst and the citrine are violet and yellow forms of quartz ; the former was the amethystus (ἀμέθυστος) of antiquity ; the latter is probably one of the stones known to Pliny under the Greek term chrysolithus.

In passing, attention may be called to one or two of the beautiful amethysts in this Collection. As specimens of large size and of the streaked and paler colours, very usual in the antique ateliers, we may mention the great pebble (No. 5) with the Serapis intaglio, and the famous Pallas of Eutyches (No. 81), the stone of which bears a strong indirect testimony to the genuineness of the work, for a modern forger would have chosen an amethyst of at least a richer hue. Quartz, crystallus (κρύσταλλος), seldom occurs with antique work upon it : a specimen of it, however, penetrated by fibres of rutile, a rare material for a gem, is here seen with a figure of the Sun God (No. 266).

We reserve the term chalcedony for the comparatively colourless varieties of the mineral ; they generally have a pale smoky yellowish or bluish hue. When coloured with any of the tints of red and yellow which the oxide of iron imparts to it, it becomes the sard (σάρδιον, sarda), so called from this word meaning yellow in Persian, not from the town of Sardis, Pliny's etymology : the pale rich yellow kind, clear yellow when looked through, and pale dull orange or brownish yellow when looked at, is the golden sard ; the yellow sard being the name for the less translucent specimens which lack the brightness of the former and have a yellower or more orange tint when looked at. The golden sard was the favourite stone of the Greek artist, who doubtless meant the work he engraved on it to be seen as a transparency. The yellow sard only occasionally carries antique work.

The sardine-stone or sardine, the *sardoine* of the French, is a dark red translucent, but sometimes very transparent, sard, the aspect of which is almost black ; its fine colour being only seen when it is looked through. It often carries noble work of the late Greek and early Imperial Roman periods; but still oftener the works of the cinque-cento and modern artists.

The " hyacinthine " sard is the term applied to a rich and glorious variety of this stone which possesses the orange-red tint, with almost the transparency of the kind of garnet termed in France " hyacinthe la belle." To these clear and beautiful kinds of sard, the writers of the last century gave the name of beryl, a term that has introduced many a case of confusion into the descriptions of gems in that century, such as the account Raspe gives of the famous Hermes (No. 165) in this Collection, which he states to be engraved on a beryl.

The duller transparent red kinds of sardine are the blood sard ; and there are varieties of the sard of every tone of red, orange, and brown, from an opaque black sard on the one hand to the pale golden kind on the other. And the sard passes by gradual steps into the cornelian, a stone from which it is, however, mineralogically distinguishable. Thus the true sard presents in its fracture a dull, hackly aspect, due probably to a microscopically-crystalline structure, not inconsistent with its very homogeneous substance, and absence of grain. It is also tougher and much harder than the cornelian, which is readily chipped, and exhibits a smooth glistening surface of fracture. The cornelian probably contains more of the opaline silica, the sard and the other chalcedonies possessing what has been termed a crypto-crystalline character, and therefore being more nearly of the nature of quartz.

In considering the other coloured varieties of chalcedony, we may next pass to those that are green. They are known by the term Plasma (a corruption, it is said, of Prasina). They present almost every tint and hue of green, yellow-green, and bluish-green, and sometimes almost rival the emerald in the beauty of the colour transmitted though them, though in translucency and lustre they can never compete with that splendid stone. Their colouring matter is usually iron, but sometimes, also, it is the chromium which gives its colour to the emerald. The chalcedony tinted by nickel, the chrysoprase of mineralogy, if it ever occurs with antique work, which is extremely doubtful, certainly only does so very rarely. It is rare, indeed, to meet with gems on plasma, the transparency and homogeneity of which are not spoilt by flaws and flecks throughout their substance. The jaspis of the Romans probably included some of the less translucent varieties. " Viret et sæpe tralucet iaspis, etiam victa multis antiquitatis gloriam retinens," is Pliny's introduction to the species of jaspis. Undoubtedly the " antiquitatis gloria " must allude to the habitual use of the green jasper, for gems and for ornaments, by the Egyptians and Phœnicians of the eld. They, however, very rarely employed the translucent kinds of stone, through which the green jasper passes into the plasma The expression " sæpe tralucet " shows that translucency was not the essential characteristic of the jaspis, as advocated by some authors. Some of the more transparent and richly tinted varieties of the plasma fell certainly among the species of the smaragdus of Pliny. Probably the ἴασπις of the Greeks included the same varieties of stone as Pliny's " iaspis "; but no Greek work that can certainly be attributed to the better periods of art is known upon any of these materials. A few archaic Greek works are, however, certainly known on a translucent plasma ; but the stone came first into general use and fashion during the early Imperial epoch, when good Imperial portraits were engraved on it. A little later it became a very common material for gems, and generally carries work remarkable for the beauty of the drawing and design, but of rather coarse workmanship in the details. These gems probably, if we may judge from the subjects common on them, belong chiefly to the period between Titus and the Antonines. Indeed, the Venus Victrix on the coins of that time is so frequent a subject on the plasma, as to suggest the idea that it may have been worn as a talisman or charm by the gentler sex (see No. 124).

A pale and delicate bluish chalcedony is that known as the sapphirine chalcedony. Heads and figures of Jove are not very uncommon upon it. An amethystine and a rose-tinted variety, the former usually with Asiatic work, are also occasionally met with.

Of the stones that we recognise by the name of jasper, which are chalcedonies charged with a sufficient amount of foreign matter to render them opaque, and which present a beautiful variety and vividness in their colours, none except the black or brownish-black varieties seem to have been employed by the Greeks, though in Roman Imperial times the other varieties came into vogue.

The Egyptians, indeed, as already mentioned, were partial to a dark-green jasper, owing its colour to the mineral chlorite, and Phœnician scarabæi are usually formed of this stone, some kinds of which are very soft, from their containing an excessive amount of this ingredient, or of the mineral termed "green earth." A pale-green jasper, that composing the material of the singular gem in this Collection (No. 46), was also sometimes used by the Egyptians for their inlaid gold *cloisonnée* work; but as materials for gems of a good period of the art, these green varieties of jasper are very rare.

Of the dark-green jasper there are two other kinds: the bloodstone is an opaque, and the heliotrope is a translucent variety which, in fact, is a dark plasma: both are characterised by red or sometimes yellow opaque stains or spots. All these stones were employed during the decline of the art in the second century—being favourite stones for astrological and gnostic subjects; the Sun God, with radiate crown and whip in hand, and often in a chariot, being frequently found engraved on them.

The vermilion-coloured jasper—"hæmatitis" of Pliny, and not to be confounded with our hæmatite, which is the native oxide of iron, though this is the colouring matter of the red jasper—is unknown as a gem stone before the Imperial Roman era had set in; in fact, Greek work on it probably does not exist. A few fine antique gems are known engraved on it, but in the best of them there is a coarseness of manipulation and finish that generally reveals the fact that they were worked by the wheel at the time when it was superseding all the other tools of the engraver. This period was probably about the reign of Trajan. The design on the red jasper is generally more stiff than on the plasma, which seems to have preceded it by some years in the fashions at Rome. The head of Vespasian (No. 441) in this Collection is probably a contemporary work, and a very ea.. example o this material; but when we come to the days of Hadrian, and more particularly of his Antonine successors, the red jasper often carries Imperial portraits with the characteristics of the work of those times. The influence of the material on the art it embodies is interestingly exhibited in the red jasper gems. As a material it seems not susceptible of the delicacy of workmanship that the tough and grainless sard so admirably responds to, and which was the first essential in a gem stone with the Greek artist. The lines have therefore to be coarser on the jasper; but on the other hand, its duller and more earthy lustre befits this coarser work and sets it off well, while, from the brilliant colour of the stone, the effect of none of the work on the red variety is lost. On the green stones, and this is particularly true of the plasmas, the duller hue, 'or rather the greater absorption of light and illuminating colours by the stone, prevents the details and modelling of the work on these stones from being well seen, unless by a lens or in strong light; and this has probably been the cause that while the engraver usually drew his outlines with freedom and artistic expression on the plasmas, the work with which the details are put in on them is so often sketchy and almost rude. And if the Greek preferred a transparent stone in general, that his work might be enjoyed as a transparency, the Roman gem-engraver seems to have wrought with a view to the effect of his work when seen directly by reflected light. Probably, with both the, so to say, business use of the gem for forming an impression was considered as of less importance in the artistic point of view than its being an object of admiration as an ornament. In many cases, again, it was neither as a signet nor as an ornament so much as in the character of a talisman that a gem was worn : and for this it was only necessary that a certain subject should be engraved on a particular stone. The silent language of Art had little power to persuade or elevate where superstitions like those of the Orphic school of mystics had dominated the reason and sealed the senses.

And to this cause, as much as to any other, is due the decline of the gem-engraver's art, even while other and kindred arts had made much less progress towards their eclipse.

The onyx, sardonyx, and banded agate are forms of agate; and agate is chalcedonic silica, deposited in successive layers, in general, in the interior of the hollows that occur in trap rocks. The deposits that have thus lined and gradually filled these hollows, must have been formed by an intermittent action, as the outline, and often the colour and other characters, of each are distinct. They seem to have been produced by an infiltration—thus inter-mittent—of silicious waters into the hollow; the silica depositing itself over the walls of the cavity, or collecting round some nucleus within it. The result is a solid mass of silica, built up of layers nearly parallel to each other, and following the contortions and angles of the surface of the cavity. A section through such a mass will therefore reveal a series of parallel bands or stripes, sometimes angular, and curved, and curiously tortuous, sometimes, however, level and nearly straight, like the stripes of a ribbon. The layers or bands in these stones present different properties. Thus in the same stone some of the layers may have the quality of sard, and like that stone, be somewhat porous; others, again, being colourless or white, and resisting infiltration. The layers of the former kind have, in some cases, been in-filtrated by the weak solution of iron salts occurring in the water that has permeated the rock, and have either become subsequently coloured by the iron oxide, through exposure to the air, or needed only the application of heat to develop in them the red or yellow hues of the sard. To such, again, as have not been thus naturally and *thoroughly* tinted, artificial colour may be imparted by the absorption of colouring solutions of iron or other metals, or of honey, and by a subsequent treatment by sulphuric and other acids, or by heat.

This art has particularly been practised in Germany, near Oberstein, where a more porous and inferior kind of agate is met with. The hills of Malwa have from the earliest days, and those of Uruguay have in quite recent times, supplied the finer kinds rich in their layers of true sard. The layers of the inferior sorts belong to a variety of chalcedony, more allied to the cornelian than to the sard.

The level and flatly laminated agates may be cut either parallel to or transversely to the direction of the strata. The so-called onyxes and sardonyxes of the gem-engraver are the stones produced by the former method : the long, oval formed, "banded" or "tri-coloured" agates (No. 257 of this Collection), on which so many of the fine Etruscan and later Greek works are engraved, are the transversely cut specimens. The term agate is usually retained for those more irregular varieties of stone in which the layers present angularities in their outlines.

The (achates) agate of Pliny, no doubt, was also applied to the less transparent of these and to the more variegated kinds of jasper; the term onyx among the ancients having been used in different senses at diverse times. Our "banded agate" represents, perhaps, the ὀνύχιον of the Greeks, the more transparent of the fantastic and irregular agates being the onyx of the Romans; though the term seems also to have been used for varieties of the sardonyx, the layers of which were not sard. A sardonyx (σαρδῷος ὄνυξ), however, was certainly a stone in which the strata lay superposed, and in which one layer at least was sard.

Much confusion has been introduced into modern descriptions of gems by the different senses in which the terms onyx and sardonyx have been used. One fashion confines the term onyx to the two-layered stones, and that of sardonyx to those in which more than two layers are superposed, irrespective of their quality.

In the descriptions in the following Catalogue, the term onyx will be used to imply a stone in which chalcedonic layers of various hues and kinds are superposed, provided none of these be of the sard character. Where one of these is sard, the stone will be termed a sardonyx. Practically, the two terms are difficult of very exact discrimination; as for instance, where the sard-like layers are of inferior or opaque quality; in the last case, the stone passes into a jasper onyx.

But in all ambiguous cases the descriptions given of each stone will render a more exact terminology unnecessary.

The sardonyx has always been the favourite material for cameos. The artists of the Ptolemaic period probably first used its differently coloured layers—at least, of the two-layered stones—in order to impart a contrast to the different surfaces of their designs. The exaggerated use of this artifice in stones with several differently tinted layers belongs to the Roman period; its effect was to produce a strong and conventional, rather than a pleasing contrast.

The term nicolo—abbreviated from onyculo—is applied to a variety, generally two-layered, of the onyx; the base layer being usually an opaque black jasper, sometimes artificially blackened; sometimes also a dark sard, while the very thin surface layer is of a pale bluish-white hue, due partly to the white of the upper layer not being pure, and partly to the effect of the black stratum below it being dimly seen through the translucent substance of this thin upper layer. Work of an earlier time than the Augustan age, on the nicolo, is probably not known; but from that time onwards it carries fair but rarely very good work, generally characterised by a certain clumsiness in the drawing and by inferior character in the treatment. The works on it were done to present a pictorial effect, the thin bluish upper layer being cut through to the dark base layer of the stone; so that the design is seen in black on a bluish-white ground. To give effect to the design—thus, dark on a white ground—a certain exaggeration in outline became necessary; just as, had the white layer been that employed to represent the subject, a more attenuated outline would be found to be required.

The nicolo continued to be a rather favourite stone, so long as gem engraving existed as an art; and among the gems of the Sassanian Dynasty in the Parthian Empire we find mingled with many luminous and lovely sards and with transcendent garnets, nicolos presenting the finest contrasts in their colours; all these stones carrying the singular and rudely worked subjects which seemed to have represented an art inherited from the days of Mesopotamian cylinders and Persian conical stamps, but modified in its *technique* by the introduction of methods, especially the use of a coarse wheel, from the West.

This stone may have been the Ægyptilla of Pliny, "nigrâ radice, cœruleâ facic."

The interesting cameo, No. 4 in this Catalogue, representing the Jupiter Axur, known also on the famous intaglio with the inscription NEICOY at St. Petersburg; the Omphale, also in cameo, on the historically interesting *double* nicolo (No. 316), composed of a black stratum between two bluish-white strata, and perforated by the original Indian boring; the huge stone with its strange African representation of the Lybian Astarte (No. 256); may be instanced among the remarkable ancient nicolos in the Marlborough Collection.

Next in importance and frequency to the large family of chalcedonic stones comes the mineralogical group known under the name of garnet, the ἄνθραξ of the Greek, and carbunculus of the Roman writers. Not to complicate the subject by mineralogical details, the garnets used by the gem engravers may be divided according to their colour. The pure transcendently red varieties, without tints of orange on the one hand, or of violet on the other, when seen by transmitted light, and known by various names, such as Bohemian garnet (slightly brownish in its hue), Syrian garnet, so called from Syriam, the capital of Pegu, and pyrope, form for our purpose one division: a second will be made up of the kinds inclining to orange when examined by transmitted light. These orange varieties, when toned with brown, and of the tint of Tavel, or tawny port wine, are the "guarnacino" garnets of the Italians. Those kinds in which the orange tends to an aurora red, are the hyacinthine garnet—the hyacinths of the jewellers. They are identical in colour with, but less lustrous than, the true hyacinth or red jacinth, which is a zircon. Often they exhibit paler and more yellow hues, and are internally seen to be full of striæ and bubble-like impurities: these are the cinnamon stone. They are doubtless one of the kinds of chrysolithus that were admired in Imperial Rome; and fine work of the Imperial age, and sometimes beautifully drawn and modelled Greek art, are met with on them.

The next variety of the garnets—thus classed according to their colours—is the kind which exhibits a violet hue mixed with the red when the stone is seen by transmitted light. They are the Oriental garnets of the jewellers, India furnishing some of the best of them. They are also called the almandine garnets, possibly from the ancient term *alabandici*, as applied to a variety of the carbunculus worked at and exported from Alabanda, in Caria. The modern term carbuncle applies to any kind of garnet that is cut "en

B

cabochon." Fair work on this lovely stone, the almandine, is not rare in the Roman period. There is generally a sort of characteristic roughness and want of polish in the interior of the designs on this stone in ancient times, contrasting curiously with the finer polish, which again corresponds often with a higher quality in the work, on the guarnacino, and hyacinthine, and cinnamon (or essonite) garnets of the epoch of Imperial Rome, or of the late Greek art that existed just before that epoch. The pretty gem (No. 27) representing Neptune is a fine example of ancient work on this stone. No. 229 is also a beautiful example of Roman work on it. Of the hyacinthine garnet we have examples in Nos. 43 and 330 ; while No. 123 is a garnet of the quality known as the Syrian or Syriam garnet, with work that seems Roman in date upon it. No. 728 may be another gem also of Roman workmanship, on a similar stone, one worthy of comparison with that in which the famous Sirius (No. 270) is sunk.

Lapis lazuli, the sapphirus (σάπφειρος) of antiquity, is a stone on which Greek and Roman work of every age—unless, perhaps, of the earliest (archaic) Greek time—is met with. Yet, though thus wide in its horizon—to use a geological phrase—it seems never to have been a common material for gems. The Mercury (No. 176) and the Hercules and Iole cameo (No. 319) will serve to illustrate the use of this material at two different periods ; and both are fine examples of the stone.

Among the rarer stones employed by the ancients, of which examples are to be met with in this Collection, the sapphire—the hyacinthus of Roman authors—is the hardest, and is among the scarcest to be met with. The Medusa (No. 98), and the head of Caracalla (No. 485), are remarkable illustrations of the stone, and of the mastery the Roman artists had acquired over its stubborn material. The beryl (beryllus), a less rare stone in antiquity than the sapphire, and, like it, Oriental in one at least of its sources, is well illustrated in the Neptune (No. 25) and the Hippocampus (No. 734), both, it may be observed, marine subjects—a class for which this material was often employed by the ancients.

The Julia Domna (No. 484), the Bacchus (No. 183), and the Gryllus (No. 690) are also excellent and very interesting examples of antique work on the beryl, a stone in which the Blenheim Collection is thus seen to be especially rich.

Of the ruby, the emerald, and the peridot, the Collection contains no antique specimens.

The turquoise is represented by a gem of singular beauty, the Livia and Tiberius cameo (No. 403). Pliny speaks of the callaina as having the hue of the topazius (our peridot), only being opaque. This is exactly the tint and character of this green turquoise—the favourite variety with the Romans. Of the blue variety, no doubt the callais, the little cameo (No. 432) seems to be an authentic antique specimen.

In this Catalogue, whenever a gem has been identified with one in the collection of Lord Bessborough, as catalogued by Natter, a reference is given to his published catalogue with the number in it of the gem. The gem-acquired from the collections of Lord Chesterfield and of Medina, are severally distinguished by the letters C and M, and by numbers also referring to the published catalogue of Natter. Similar references are given to the gems that can be identified with those described in the catalogue of the Arundel Collection, as it stood in Lady Elizabeth Germain's time. A reference is occasionally made to a catalogue already alluded to—drawn up by the third Duke—which was probably intended ultimately for publication. But in general when no reference is made to the Bessborough or Arundel collections, the gem was one of those collected by the third Duke himself. The descriptions given by his Grace of the Bessborough and Arundel gems are those of Natter's, or of the Arundelian Catalogue, of which he must have possessed a copy ; and they are but little altered. Raspe's catalogue of Tassie's casts has also, of course, been among the many works ransacked to trace the history of the gems.

In using the phrase "to the right," or "to the left," as applied to a head or bust, the direction is that of the head on the gem itself as seen by the spectator, not that on the cast from it. The terms "confronted" and "conjoined" are used respectively for faces represented as looking towards each other, or as looking the same way where one is partly eclipsed by the other.

The term "conjugated" will be reserved for cases in which heads are united, as in the Companion coins of Janus, or as in the caprices and medleys of masks, so common upon gems.

Inscriptions on the intaglios are to be considered as retrograde, unless described as being otherwise.

CATALOGUE.

First Day's Sale.

On MONDAY, JUNE 26, 1899,

AT ONE O'CLOCK PRECISELY.

I. MYTHOLOGY

SECTION I.—THE GODS.

(1.) *THE TWELVE GREAT OLYMPIAN DIVINITIES.*

Zeus—Jupiter.

1 INTAGLIO. A HEAD OF JOVE, to the left, on hæmatite. A Roman work of fine execution

2 AN INTAGLIO ON A RED SARD, representing Jupiter standing holding a long sceptre in his right hand ; his eagle in the field
An Arundel gem (Cat. Th. A, No. 40)

3 AN INTAGLIO HEAD OF JUPITER AMMON, to the left, on a sard highly foiled. A bold Roman work, resembling the head on some of the Consular coins. In gold ring, the back enamelled
A Bessborough gem (N. Cat. No. 19 c) *originally in the Collection of Lord Chesterfield. Figured by Worlidge*

4 CAMEO CUT IN A NICOLO, once covered with a film of brown, which is reserved to form a rim, and also survives on the paludamentum and eagle's wing. The beardless Jupiter, Jupiter axur, a full-length figure, standing with the thunderbolt and sceptre, and the eagle in the field. The Ægis envelops his loins. The work is indubitably ancient, and probably represents an emperor, perhaps Augustus himself, as Jove. This figure is that designated as St. John the Evangelist in mediæval times. The famous intaglio at St. Petersburg, signed NEICOY, is similar in its subject

A gem from the Arundel Collection (Cat. Th. D, 13)

[Jupiter Serapis, &c.] Nos. 5 to 11.

5 AN INTAGLIO CUT ON THE BOSS OF A LARGE PEBBLE OF AMETHYST, polished in its original shape. A front-faced head of Jupiter Serapis. It is Roman or Romano-Egyptian work of the finest type; the stone is 1½ inch in diameter

One of the Bessborough gems (N. Cat. No. 14)

6 INTAGLIO HEAD OF JUPITER SERAPIS, represented in full face, cut out of the black upper layer of a jasper onyx, of which the base layer is white. It is work of the second century

An Arundel gem (Cat. Th. A, No. 3)

7 INTAGLIO HEAD OF JUPITER SERAPIS, full face, on a plasma of rich colour

An Arundel gem (Cat. Th. A, No. 2)

8 A MINUTE INTAGLIO, representing Jupiter Serapis enthroned; a sceptre is in his hand, the modius on his head, and Cerberus by his side. It is engraved in the yellow upper layer of a sardonyx, exhibiting also a white stratum, under which is a black base layer. The whole figure is not much above ¼ inch in length

9 INTAGLIO HEAD OF SERAPIS, to the left; a Roman work of the minutest dimensions, cut on an oval sardonyx, bevelled away to exhibit a yellowish-brown top layer, which is separated from a greyish-black base by a broad white band. It is a counterpart of the Isis (No. 45), but the colours of the stone are even more brilliant

10 AN INTAGLIO OF THE RENAISSANCE PERIOD, cut in a pale sapphirine chalcedony, and representing, in very rude workmanship, Serapis enthroned between Isis and Pallas within a Zodiac, carried by Atlas

11 CONFRONTED HEADS OF SERAPIS AND ISIS; an intaglio of Roman work, on a yellowish sard

A Bessborough gem, from the Chesterfield Collection (N. Cat. No. 27 c)

12 AN ONYX CAMEO, representing in profile the heads of Zeus and Hera, both to the right. A fine Greek work, cut in a translucent white layer, backed by an understratum of bluish-grey

A Bessborough gem (N. Cat. 26)

Figured in the " Marlborough Gems," vol. i. No. 29

13 A CAMEO ON A TWO-LAYERED SARDONYX; the subject a fine head of Jupiter, ¾ face, looking to the right. It is cut in a white stratum overlying a black base layer

An Arundel gem (Cat. Th. B, 31)

14 A CAMEO HEAD OF JUPITER, to the right, on a superb five-layered sardonyx. The uppermost layer, of a pale cinnamon hue, is reserved to form a rim. Under a white layer in which the head is cut is another brown stratum, below which second white layer is seen resting on a base of black sard. The stone is bevelled to exhibit the beauty of its strata

4

Associations and Attributes of Zeus.

15 AN INTAGLIO ON A SARDONYX, representing Zeus Gigantomachos, signed ΑΘΗΝΙΩΝ. It is cut in a brownish-red upper layer, below which are seen a white stratum and a base of dark grey. It is a fine work, and worthy of the stone, the layers of which are very equal in thickness

[**Europa.**]

16 AN INTAGLIO ON YELLOWISH CHALCEDONY, representing Europa and Jove in the character of a Bull
A *Bessborough gem* (*N. Cat. No.* 109)

[**Leda.**]

17 INTAGLIO ON A DARK SARDINE. Leda and the Jove-swan, by Pichler

18 A VERY SMALL CAMEO OF LEDA WITH THE JOVE-SWAN BY HER SIDE. Excellent Roman work on onyx
An Arundel gem (*Cat. Thee. A. No.* 136)

19 THE SAME SUBJECT ON A CAMEO OF ONYX
An Arundel gem (*Cat. Th. A.* 144)

[**Ganymede.**]

20 AN INTAGLIO ON A DARK SARD. The eagle soaring with Ganymede. It is inscribed ΚΟΙΝΟΥ
Bought by the Duke who formed the Collection, from Cipriani; and figured in the "Marlborough Gems," col. ii. 42

21 AN INTAGLIO HEAD OF GANYMEDE, to the right, with the eagle introduced as a minute symbol in the field. It is a work of Burch, unsurpassed in finish, upon a superb sardonyx of three layers. The surface layer of a pale chestnut is cut away, except where it forms a reserved rim. The next layer of bluish-white carries the intaglio, and under it is a base layer of deep brown sard. The beautiful strata of the stone are shown by its being bevelled, while from the depth of the reserved rim the impression stands out like a medallion. The gem carries the signature of the artist

22 A VERY FINE CAMEO ON AN ONYX, representing a head of Gauy-
mede, to the right, in a Phrygian cap. The relief is in a
porcelain-white layer, the base consisting of a horn-like
stratum. It is a work very antique in its character

23 A ROMAN CAMEO OF THE FINE IMPERIAL TIME, on sardonyx, in
a bluish-white layer. Ganymede feeding the eagle of Jove.
A dark sard stratum forms the base of the stone
It was an Arundel gem (Cat. Th. B, 44), and is figured,
" Marlborough Gems," vol. ii. 43

Hera—Juno.

24 A SMALL FULL-LENGTH FIGURE OF JUNO, on a fine nicolo.
She holds a sceptre, and in one hand a conical object. It is
good work of Imperial Roman age
A Bessborough gem, once Lord Chesterfield's. Natter (Cat.
34 c) calls it Liberalitas

Poseidon—Neptune.

25 AN INTAGLIO, representing Neptune in full-length figure on a
beryl, a stone so often devoted by the antique artist to mari-
time subjects. As in the Neptune of Cenchreæ and that on
the coins of Demetrius Poliorcetes, his left hand holds a
dolphin, in his right is the trident, and his left foot rests on
the prow of a ship. In the exergue are the letters GLAVI
(probably the owner's name). It is good probably Roman
work, and finished with the " diamond point "
An Arundel gem (Cat. Thec. A, 42)

26 AN INTAGLIO OF NEPTUNE, somewhat similar in position and
in attributes to the preceding. It is engraved in a nicolo,
and appears to be a work of rather late Roman date

27 AN INTAGLIO ON A CONVEX ALMANDINE, represents Neptune in
figure similar to the last, but without the dolphin. There is
a hydra on the rock on which the right foot rests. It is a
large and finely cut gem of apparently an early Imperial
Roman date. Set in gold as a seal

    A Bessborough gem (numbered in Natter's Catalogue, 47)

28 AN INTAGLIO ON A SARD, representing a bust of Neptune, to the
left. It is fine Greek work

    It was figured by Worlidge, in his Etchings of Gems, No. 31

Associations, Attributes, &c., of Poseidon.

29 INTAGLIO ON A RED CORNELIAN, in which Neptune and Amphitrite
are seen riding on a sea-horse

    An Arundel gem (Cat. Th. A, No. 31)

30 HEAD OF A TRITON, to the left; fins are appended to the
mouth, and the beard is represented as if wet. An intaglio
of Roman work, representing a rather uncommon subject on a
jasper

31 INTAGLIO ON AN AMETHYST. A Nereid on two dolphins, holding
or reining a hippocampus,—a beautiful work. Mounted in
gold as a seal

32 A DEEPLY CUT INTAGLIO ON A WHITE CHALCEDONY OF A
TRITON AND A NEREID (AMPHITRITE?)

    An Arundel gem (Cat. Th. A, No. 32)

33 A CAMEO ON A THREE-LAYERED ONYX. A Triton and a Nymph
sport on the waves, with an elaborate background. These,
with a Triton and a hippocampus, are rendered in a white
layer of the stone, below which lie a bluish and a horn-like
stratum

    A Bessborough gem (N. Cat. No. 27)

34 A MINUTE RIVER-GOD RECLINING: an intaglio on a jasper onyx.
It is somewhat deeply cut in the black surface layer; a white
and a black stratum are seen on the bevelled edge of the gem.
Mounted as a seal

    An Arundel gem (Cat. Th. A, No. 91)

35 AN ONYX CAMEO, representing a river-god in an opaque white
layer on a black ground

*A Bessborough gem, being one of those purchased from
Medina of Leghorn (Cat. No. 22 M)*

Demeter—Ceres.

36 A CAMEO ON SARDONYX. It represents a head of Demeter, to
the right, in fine Greek or Greco-Roman work. The face is
rendered in a white porcelain layer, the hair in one of coffee-
brown colour, under these is a bottom layer of black jasper.
In the hair is wreathed a chaplet of poppies, and over the
head is a veil

37 A VEILED HEAD AND BUST OF CERES, in very high relief, cut in
cameo out of a beautiful amethyst. In gold border, pierced
and enamelled .

A Bessborough gem (Cat. No. 10)
See Illustration, p. 39

Associations, &c., of Demeter.

38 AN ONYX CAMEO WITH A REPRESENTATION OF CERES SEATED
AND HOLDING A CORNUCOPIA. Triptolemus before her, pre-
senting what appears to be wheat-ears, leans on the *rutrum*.
A column with an urn fills up the design. Mr. King con-
ceives the gem to bear a flattering allusion to Germanicus;
Livia and Germanicus being frequently thus represented.
The stone is 1¾ inch high; the figures are carved in a porce-
lain-white layer lying on a stratum of brown sard

An Arundel gem (Cat. Th. D, 15)
See Illustration, p. 48

39 ABUNDANTIA, a head, to the right, and bust with a cornucopia
in her left hand, in intaglio of unusually good work, on bronze

40 AN INTAGLIO OF VERY GOOD ROMAN WORKMANSHIP ON A FINE
SARD : its subject is Abundantia, full-length figure; wheat-
ears in one hand, a dish of fruit in the other; an ant in the
field

41 A Singular "Eyed" Agate, carrying an intaglio of Roman workmanship, representing Vertumnus or Bonus Eventus in a small full-length figure, nude, with wheat-ears in one hand, and a patera in the other

A Bessborough gem (Cat. No. 60)

42 An Intaglio on Cornelian. Bonus Eventus carrying grapes and wheat-ears

An Arundel gem (Cat. Th. A, No. 95)

[Isis, &c.]

43 Isis, or rather an Egyptian Queen, to the left, in the character of Isis, with the persea fruit on her head ; cut in intaglio on a beautiful hyacinthine garnet. It is probably Egyp.-Roman, but may belong to the Ptolemaic period

A Bessborough gem (N. Cat. 94). Natter calls the stone a Hyacintho Quarnacino, and adds " il se nomme aussi Berill ; on appelle Berill toutes les pierres rouges ou jaunes, quand elles sont d'une couleur bien unie et bien transparente ; ceux qui sont d'un rouge foncé sont nommés Hyacinthi Quarnacini ;" a remark which explains the peculiar use of the terms Beryl, Hyacinth, and Guarnacino garnet, during the last century. This was a gem of the Chesterfield Collection

44 An Intaglio of Isis in a Full-length Figure, cut on a convex garnet

A purchase of the third Duke's

45 Isis Suckling Horus. An intaglio of the same minute dimensions as the Serapis No. 9, the drawing of both being excellent. It is on a similar sardonyx ; the surface layer in which the engraving is cut is yellowish-brown, beneath is a white stratum on a base layer of dark bluish-grey jasper

46 Isis : A FEMALE HEAD, of very Hebrew physiognomy, to the left; an intaglio, on the pale green jasper often used in ancient Egyptian ornaments. On the head is the Vulture head-dress, but devoid of the head of the bird : on the neck is an Egyptian necklace. The subject and the *carresque* character of the engraving would point to an Egyptian origin for this elaborate gem. The treatment of the details, which are not of Ptolemaic character, would indicate a date for the work not earlier than the Romano-Egyptian period. Mr. King supposes it to be a portrait and even the signet of Cleopatra herself! But the Vulture attire invariably has, in the earlier times, the head and neck of the Vulture rising from the brow —or this head attire is replaced by the asp's head—in the authentic portraits of Egyptian queens and goddesses of whom it is the attribute. Moreover, while the nose and face of this gem represent the conventional features of Isis, they are very unlike those of Cleopatra as rendered on coins. On the reverse is an Egyptian distyle temple, having in its centre the head and bust of Hathor. A precisely similar gem on the same material is figured by Tassie as a cameo, and stated to have been the property of the Marquis Capponi at Rome. It probably is this gem ; the place of which in the Blenheim Collection was among those acquired by the third Duke of Marlborough

Apollo.

47 INTAGLIO ON A FINE RED SARD. A head of Apollo, to the left. Fine work, apparently by a Greek artist

A Bessborough gem. Natter in his Catalogue (No. 80) *calls it a " Berill très bien travaillé "*

48 INTAGLIO ON A DULL RED SARD, of the head of Apollo, to the left, a sprig of bay in the field

gem among the Chesterfield portion of the Bessborough Collection (No. 16 c *in Natter's Catalogue)*

49 INTAGLIO ON A DARK RED SARD. The same subject as the last, to the left

> Probably the Arundel gem termed "Pacis caput" (Cat. Th. A, 25)

50 INTAGLIO, ON A RED SARD, OF APOLLO PLAYING THE LYRE: a fine Greek gem of considerable size

> An Arundel gem: the Apollo Citharœdus incidens of the Arundel Catalogue (Th. A, 45)

51 A MAGNIFICENT GEM, like the last in attitude and subject—Apollo Musagetes—with the chlamys falling nearly to the feet. It is a Greek work of noble simplicity

> An Arundel gem (Th. A, 45)

53 A VERY BEAUTIFUL MODERN INTAGLIO, on a fine sard. It represents Apollo much in the attitude of the "Belvedere"

54 AN INTAGLIO, representing Apollo with his bow and a spread chlamys, cut in a fine jasper agate stone, banded with brown and white

> An Arundel gem (Cat. Thec. E, No. 27)

55 INTAGLIO ON A FINE SARD. A head to the left, probably of Apollo. It is a fine gem, that might have been wrought in Magna Græcia. The hair falls in beautifully worked curls, and the face is of the true Greek type

56 A DEEPLY-CUT INTAGLIO. Apollo tuning his lyre; on a nicolo of great beauty. It was a Bessborough gem

57 INTAGLIO ON A FINE TRANSPARENT SARD. The "placable" Apollo (as on coins of the Seleucidœ) holds downwards the arrow with his right hand, the bent bow being in his left

58 INTAGLIO ON A SARD. Apollo Citharœdus; in the field an altar.

> An Arundel gem (Cat. Th. A, No. 44)

59 A SMALL INTAGLIO, on a fine oval sard, that has been somewhat polished down. A nude figure, apparently of Apollo, stands in the middle of the gem ; on his head is a somewhat conical object, and in his hand he holds what may be a mask. His lyre, on the ground, rests against a tree on which sits a bird like a crow. On the other side is also a tree, with a similar bird upon it ; and on its stem a female head appears as though part of the tree: perhaps Daphne, or Apollo's favourite Cyparissus, pining away into cypress out of grief for the slaughter of a favourite stag ; or it may be only a comic mask. Beneath this tree is a hind suckling an infant (Telephus?)

60 AN INTAGLIO CUT IN A SHALLOW MANNER IN A BEAUTIFUL GOLDEN SARD, of fine but late Greek work.

Apollo mourning the death of Coronis. The youthful god, loosely robed in the chlamys, leans against a tree, and mournfully contemplates the lifeless figure of the maiden, whom he slew on the accusation of a crow. The crow sits on a rock over her. Winckelmann ("Monum. inediti ") calls this group Achilles mourning the death of Penthesilea

A Bessborough gem (Cat. No. 37), on " Berill," says Natter. Figured in the " Marlborough Gems," vol. ii. 40.

61 A CAMEO ON A SARDONYX, perhaps a Roman gem, reworked in later time, representing a laureated bust of Apollo to the right. The face is worked in a white stratum, the wreath and part of the robe being in brown surface layer on a dark base ; backed with gold

See Illustration, p. 20

62 A CAMEO HEAD OF APOLLO, to the right, somewhat in the garb of a Muse ; the hair, which is laureated, is done in a fine rich brown layer of a sardonyx, the face in a white layer, a translucent greyish-black material forming the base. The profile is beautiful, but effeminate, and Greek in character. The gem is 1¾ inch high by $1\frac{1}{16}$ inch.

63 HEAD OF APOLLO, laureated, to the left, on an onyx. The head
is in a bluish-white layer on a black ground.

*One of the Medina gems in the Bessborough Collection (Cat.
No. 16 M)*

64 A PASTE CAMEO OF APOLLO'S HEAD, to the right

Associations, &c., of Apollo,

65 A BEAUTIFUL INTAGLIO ON A SARD. A bust of Clio, to the right,
with the historic roll of papyrus in her hand. It is figured
in Worlidge

*An Arundel gem, called in the Catalogue (Th. E. 23)
"Semiramis—the roll representing her dagger. It has the
same attribution in the "Marlborough Gems," where it is
figured, vol. i. 26*

66 A MUSE, to the left. Intaglio on a sard

67 AN INTAGLIO ON A FINE, LONG OVAL CORNELIAN. Terpsichore
tuning her lyre. By her a cippus carrying a statue of Pallas

68 A MODERN INTAGLIO ON A FINE GOLDEN SARD. Melpomene
holding a mask ; a cippus behind her

69 AN INTAGLIO ON A VERY FINE PLASMA. Melpomene holding
a mask ; a cippus behind her ; in the field a shield and a
falchion

*An Arundel gem, designated in the Catalogue (Th. A, 60)
as "Tomyris Scytharum regina," the mask standing for the head
of Cyrus, and the falchion for the weapon of her vengeance*

70 INTAGLIO ON A FINE SARD, representing the head and bust of a
Muse, to the left. The letters ΣΑΦ have been scratched in
at some later period. The lyre is introduced in the field
with a bee

Artemis—Diana.

71 An Intaglio Head of Artemis, to the right, with the end of her
quiver showing over her shoulder ; on a brown sard ; it is
a large and curious gem of early workmanship
An Arundel gem (Cat. Th. E, 7)

72 A Head of Artemis, to the right. A cameo upon a fine
sardonyx ; the hair arranged with the κρώβυλος is rendered
in a very dark brown sard upper layer, one curl however
being yellow ; the face, in a layer of ivory-white, is relieved
by a fine sard background

73 A Full-length Standing Figure of Diana Holding Out an
Arrow, a cippus behind her ; an intaglio in a beautiful
hyacinthine sard. The work is exceedingly good

74 Diana Leaning on a Pillar, a stag in the field, on a fine transparent yellowish sard
An Arundel gem (Cat. Th. A, 57)

75 Intaglio on a Sardonyx. The "Diana of the Hills." It is
signed ΑΠΟΛΛΩΝΙΟΥ. It is cut in a layer of orange-red
sard, below which lie two strata of white and brown
A Bessborough gem ; Natter's Diana Montana (Cat. 100)

Hephaistos—Vulcan.

77 An Intaglio on a Beautiful Agate. Vulcan at work shaping
a helmet
A Bessborough gem (Cat. No. 103)

78 An Italian Intaglio on a Cornelian. Vulcan's workshop, with
a great many figures. The setting is one of a series in the
Collection exhibiting a delicately pencilled and richly coloured
pattern of tulips and other flowers painted on a white ground
An Arundel gem (Cat. Thec. E, No. 1)

C

79 AN INTAGLIO ON CORNELIAN. " Vulcan seated, a veiled lady by him; gives the sword and shield to a youthful warrior"; beneath the feet of Vulcan ΑΔΜΩΝ. Dr. Brunn considers it to be a copy from an Alban sarcophagus, with the Marriage of Peleus and Thetis (Millin. Gal. Myth. t. 152, n. 551)

A Bessborough gem ; described by Natter (Cat. No. 95),
who omits to mention the signature, as Brutus imposing an
oath on Collatinus to avenge Lucretia

Pallas Athene—Minerva.

80 A MINUTE INTAGLIO OF A HEAD OF PALLAS, by Louis Siriès, to the right, engraved with the point alone on a yellow sard. The gem is let into a small rim of ivory-white chalcedony

81 BUST OF PALLAS, full face ; a deeply cut intaglio in a large pale amethyst. It carries the signature

EYTYXHC
ΔΙΟCΚΟΥΡΙΔΟΥ
ΑΙΓΙΑΙΟC ΕΠ.

This noble intaglio must be held to be the original of one of the most interesting of antique signed gems, and to bear the autograph of a son of perhaps the great Dioscorides. The engraving, though not of high finish, is of the boldest character. It is figured in the "Marlborough Gems," vol. ii. No. 12

82 BUST OF PALLAS, to the right, in intaglio on yellowish chalcedony. Of the Roman period
An Arundel gem (Th. E, 8)

83 PALLAS, A BUST IN INTAGLIO, to the right, on a fine sard agate. The stone is a beautiful one of the Oriental kind
An Arundel gem (Cat. Thec. V, No. 17)

84 A CAMEO BUST OF PALLAS, to the left, on a three-layered onyx. The face is cut in a white layer, an upper horn-like stratum forming the helmet; with a base layer of the same kind
A Medina gem (Bessborough Catalogue, No. 13 M)

85 MINERVA BUST, to the right : a cameo. Her hair is in a yellow
ish brown, her face in a white layer on a dull-coloured base.
The helmet is otherwise only represented by the plume. Good
Roman work.

An Arundel gem, termed, in the Catalogue of Lady E.
Germain, " Caput Zenobiæ" (Cat. Thec. B, 11)

86 A CAMEO ON A SARDONYX, REPRESENTING A BUST OF PALLAS, to
the left. The helmet, shoulder, and hair in a red layer, the face
in white on a red base

87 A BUST OF PALLAS, to the right, a beautiful cameo, cut upon a
stone as beautiful, a sardonyx, presenting a rich brown layer
on a white ground. The helmet is covered with a fantastic
leaf ornament, carrying a mask on the visor

An Arundel gem (Cat. Thec. C, 6)

88 A CAMEO BUST OF PALLAS, to the left, somewhat elaborate in
its workmanship. It is undercut to give effect to the profile
which is worked in a thick white layer. Mounted in a frame
set with pastes, the loop formed as a helmet and trophy

One of the gems bought by Lord Bessborough of Medina
(Cat. 36 M)

89 CAMEO BUST OF MINERVA, to the left, on a sardonyx. The
hair is rendered in a yellow layer, the face and neck in a
stratum of white upon a base layer of dull orange ; the cheek
is just tinted with a film of the surface layer. The work is
probably of the period of Hadrian.

90 ATHENE " PROMACHOS." A Roman intaglio cut in the upper layer
of a minute nicolo. A crescent in the field is probably an
astrological emblem

91 A CAMEO WITH PICHLER'S SIGNATURE, on a fine little three-layered
sardonyx, representing Athene " Promachos." Her shield
carrying an owl is left in a yellow layer ; the base layer is of
dark grey

c 2

92 Minerva in a Car Drawn by Two Owls, on a yellow cornelian ;
a pretty little Roman intaglio

93 An Intaglio on a Nicolo. A sacrifice to Minerva by a Roman
warrior, perhaps Domitian. She holds out an owl towards
him, the serpent being in the field as one of her attributes,
left hand resting on a shield

94 An Onyx Cameo. A helmeted bust of Pallas, to the right, cut out
of an ivory-white layer, on a bluish-grey ground

Figured in the " Marlborough Gems," vol. i. 27

95 A Small Head of Pallas, to the Left, helmeted, with a mask
on the helmet ; in an ivory-white layer on a bluish-grey
ground

An Arundel gem (Cat. Thec. A, 112)

Associations, Attributes, and Symbols of Pallas.*

96 The Head of Medusa (or of Perseus) in Front Face: a small
and deep intaglio on a bright golden sard. It is beautiful,
perhaps Greek work. A caduceus in the field

*Figured by Worlidge (No. 27) as a Mercury. It was a
Bessborough gem (No. 18 c in Natter's Catalogue).*

97 A Fragment of an Exquisite Cameo, representing the tranquil
Medusa, more probably Perseus, to the right ; a gem that
must once have been 1½ inch in length by 1¼ inch in diameter.
In somewhat flat though not shallow relief, the hair and the
wing are rendered in a rich brown layer ; a fine ivory white
layer of the sardonyx furnishing the material for a countenance
of severe beauty. The style is that of a fine Greek period

---

* The myth of the Gorgon Medusa being represented in connection with the
conquest of the mortal Gorgon by Perseus, and the assumption of her head by
Athene as the ornament and terror of her shield, subjects representing Medusa
Perseus, &c., are not placed in a separate division, but are included with those
which represent the attributes and associations of Athene.

No. 457.

No. 100.

98 AN INTAGLIO ON SAPPHIRE. Medusa's head, in full front face: extremely fine work, and exhibiting a wonderful finish considering the hard material in which it is worked. The wings in the hair and the serpent's crest between the wings and round the chin indicate a comparatively late period for its execution. The sapphire is of a pale colour, and is mounted in an enamelled ring of the cinque-cento period, with arabesques and black vines covering the gold of the mounting. The engraving is probably a work of a good Roman time

An Arundel gem (Cat. Thec. A, No. 1)

99 CAMEO HEAD OF THE TRANQUIL MEDUSA, to the left. It is cut in the white porcelain-like upper layer of an onyx, with a bluish-white background. The relief is not so flat as in No. 97, and the presence of the serpent in the hair, together with the wing, betokens a comparatively late date for the gem. The beautiful modelling of the features, and the fine work in the hair, would preclude a date later than that of Hadrian.

Figured in the " Marlborough Gems," col. ii. No. 10

100 A CAMEO, of proportions almost sufficient to raise it into a work of sculpture. It is a Medusa's head, in enormous relief, cut from a large homogeneous boss of translucent chalcedony. The face is turned slightly to the right, and the expression in the eyes, brows, mouth, indeed on every feature, conveys all that art could embody of the " dreadful Gorgon." Every part of the face is as delicately modelled as if the material had been as soft as marble; and Mr. King has called this gem " the noblest work in relief that graces the collection." Six holes, drilled in somewhat divergent directions from behind, some of which penetrate in a concealed manner even into the recesses of the hair on the upper surface of the gem, held the fastenings that affixed this finest known phalera to a perhaps imperial corselet. A seventh hole is sunk into the back of the stone for some depth below the nose and upper lip, evidently to give a greater transparency and life to those features. This great work belongs probably to the age of

Trajan or of Hadrian, if indeed it may not be assigned to the
Macedonian period of Greek art

*From the Bessborough Collection. Natter (in his Catalogue
No.* 1) *remarks that the right side is cut en biais (with an
inclination towards the other side), in order to give force to
the left side*

See Illustration

101 MEDUSA, to the right, a cameo of beautiful work, on a fine
cornelian

102 A PROFILE CAMEO OF MEDUSA, to the right. The hair, in which
the serpents and the wing are combined, is given in a black
surface layer; the face in one of an ivory white, backed by a
dark grey ground. It is fine work, of Hadrian's time

103 AN ONYX CAMEO: full-faced head of Medusa with wings. Set
in a massive gold ring, the bezel and shoulders elaborately
chased with masks and scrollwork in high relief, and richly
enamelled in various colours

See Illustration, p. 56

104 A FRONT-FACED MEDUSA, slightly turned ; a cameo, somewhat
deeply cut in the ivory-white upper layer of an onyx with a
dark base. In open frame setting adorned with sapphires,
peridot, &c.

From the Bessborough Collection (Cat. 5)

105 AN ONYX CAMEO OF THE MEDUSA'S HEAD, much like the last.
It is cut in a porcelain-like upper layer with a grey
background

One of the Bessborough gems (Cat. 33 M), *from the
Medina Collection*

106 A GORGON'S HEAD, full face, cameo, in flat relief, in an ivory-
white surface layer with a yellowish-brown base ; the hair is
rendered in this latter transparent under layer

An Arundel gem (Cat. Thec. A, 103), *called caput Solis*

107 PERSEUS WITH THE GORGON'S HEAD, viewing its image in his
shield, while he leans against a column. A work in shallow
cameo on a fine sardonyx.

An Arundel gem (Cat. Thec. C, 19)

108 AN INTAGLIO ON A PALE SARD, signed ΧΡΩΝΙΟΥ. Perseus, an
inverted harpè in his right hand, head of Medusa in his left.

A Bessborough gem (Cat. No. 99)

Ares—Mars.

109 AN INTAGLIO BUST, to the left, of Ares helmeted. A large intaglio, simple in its style and finely executed; its value is enhanced by its being still mounted in an antique setting consisting of a milled edge formed by the twisting together of two gold wires, which gives to the impression an appearance of an Etruscan border. It is engraved on a cornelian of large size, 1½ inch in height, and it is probably work of Greco-Roman period

From Lord Arundel's Collection (Cat. Thec. E, 26)

110 A BEAUTIFUL LITTLE GEM, representing Ares reposing. An intaglio on a yellow sard, probably the work of a Greek hand

Described as Un Soldat by Natter (Cat. No. 44 c) among the Bessborough Gems. Figured in the " Marlborough Gems," vol. i. No. 38

111 "MARS ULTOR," AN INTAGLIO ON A FINE SARD, of very excellent Roman work. In the field is the inscription MARS ULTOR

An Arundel gem (Cat. Thec. A, No. 46). It is figured in the " Marlborough Gems," vol. i. No. 37

112 MARS RESTING ON A SHIELD. Intaglio, on a sard, of Roman work. Set as seal

An Arundel gem (Cat. Thec. A, No. 86)

113 MARS, Venus approaching him, Hercules and Minerva on either side. A Roman intaglio, on a beautiful yellow sard

An Arundel gem (Cat. Thec. A, No. 33)

Aphrodite—Venus.

114 HEAD OF APHRODITE, to the left. Intaglio on a sard. A beautiful little gem of Greek workmanship

115 INTAGLIO BUST OF APHRODITE, to the left. A large gem cut in a hyacinthine garnet. The hair has been carefully worked with the "diamond point"

116 An Intaglio Bust as Aphrodite, to the left, on a bright red
sard

An Arundel gem (Cat. Thec. A, 7)

117 Venus, something in design like the " Medici," on a very fine
blood-red sard

118 Intaglio Head of Venus on a Sard

119 A Head of Venus in Profile, to the left. A large cameo on
a splendid sardonyx. The hair is partly rendered in a brown
surface layer, the features in one of opaque white on a dark
sard ground. The work is of the highest character and
finish. In gold moulded border set in open framework of
arabesque design, and mounted with peridots and amethysts.
See Illustration
One of the Medina gems (No. 29 m) *of the Bessborough
Catalogue*

120 A Pretty Little Cameo. A bust of Venus, to the right.
Carved in the white layer of an onyx, with a grey background : a finely finished and beautifully genuine Roman
work

121 A Head of Venus, to the right. A cameo in very high relief,
with a wreath, probably of myrtle, in her hair, which is
dressed in long ringlets and expressed in a surface layer of
a rich brown colour ; the features are rendered in a stratum
like ivory ; the base pearly white
Probably an Arundel gem (Ar. Cat. Thec. II. No. 30) *called
a Semiramis*

122 Venus Victrix, to the right ; or it may be, as suggested by
Mr. Newton, Artemis ; with an erect javelin in front of her.
A three-quarter length figure, cut in shallow intaglio on a
splendid sard agate. The dimensions of this magnificent
gem are nearly the same as those of two others to which in
workmanship it bears much resemblance : both are profiles
and both on similar stones to this. One of them is the fragment, the youthful Augustus in the character of Mercury,
No. 387 in this Collection. The other gem is a Pallas, a three-

No. 61.

No. 119

quarter length figure at Florence of a similarly Amazonian type with this gem. The robe, as in this gem, is of a gauzy texture. Both this and the Florentine gem are probably portraits in the characters of the deities they represent ; the attributes of those goddesses being just sufficiently expressed in the one case by the plume of the helm and by a ribbon-like adjunct of serpents to the slight drapery, while here the character of the Venus Victrix, or Artemis, is just indicated by the spear erect in the field before the figure. The features not a little resemble those of Marcia, but the work seems too good for the age of Commodus

It is figured in the "Marlborough Gems," vol. ii. No. 6, where it is called a Phryne. It was an Arundel gem (Cat. Thec. E, No. 4)

123 VENUS SEATED, HOLDING OUT A WREATH; on a fine Siriam garnet. A Roman intaglio of Imperial time
   From the Bessborough Collection (Cat. No. 46)

124 A ROMAN INTAGLIO, ON A PALE PLASMA, representing "Venus Victrix," a subject of frequent occurrence on this stone. A vase with three ears of wheat stands in the field ; while on her sword rests what may be her spear or a long flambeau surmounted by her pigeon
   From the Chesterfield part of the Bessborough Collection (Cat. No. 35 c)

125 "APHRODITE ANADYOMENE," INTAGLIO, cut in the red convex layer of an onyx with a white base

126 A SARDONYX CAMEO OF THE VENUS "ACCROUPIE," cut in an ivory-white layer on a yellowish sard base

127 A GOOD ROMAN CAMEO, representing a Venus seated and robing herself
   An Arundel gem (Cat. Thec. A. 141)

128 A SARDONYX CAMEO, VENUS WASHING HER FOOT IN A BATH. It is cut in a white layer, with a reserved rim of the same material, with a yellowish-brown base

129 VENUS, OR, PERHAPS, HERMAPHRODITUS, copied from a statue in
the Villa Borghese. A sardonyx, in which the mattress is
represented in a yellowish-brown stratum lying between a
white ground layer and a surface layer, also of white, in
which the figure is expressed

130 A CAMEO FIGURE OF VENUS, in a Renaissance setting, with rubies
and diamonds. It is cut in a clear white layer of an onyx
  One of the Medina gems in the Bessborough Collection (Cat.
  No. 34 M)

131 VENUS AT HER TOILET, with two Cupids in attendance. It is
engraved in a black and white banded agate

133 A LOVELY LITTLE CINQUE-CENTO INTAGLIO, on a garnet, of Venus
drawn by a pair of doves; Cupid extending his torch over
her from behind
  An Arundel gem (Cat. Thec. A, 59)

Associations, Attributes, &c., of Aphrodite.

134 A REMARKABLE GEM, ENGRAVED IN INTAGLIO ON QUARTZ,
backed with gold. A winged hermaphroditic figure, with an
androgynous figure not winged, and Vulcan hammering on
an anvil in the field. It is deeply cut, of an Asiatic style
of art, and is supposed by Mr. King to represent the male
form of Aphrodite, represented at Amathus as Aphroditus
  One of the Arundel gems (Cat. Thec. C, No. 23)

135 AN ANDROGYNOUS VENUS, OR A HERMAPHRODITUS, erect and unveiling himself; an intaglio on a beautiful little nicolo, of
good and minute Roman work of about the date of Hadrian

136 A CAMEO, ON 'A TWO-LAYERED SARDONYX. Hermaphroditus seated unveiling himself, cut in a white layer on a yellow sard base

An Arundel gem (Cat. Thec. A, 133)

137 A RECLINING HERMAPHRODITUS. A Cupid in the field. A cameo of the cinque-cento time, cut out of a porcelain white layer resting on a black base

Eros, and the Erotic Cycle.

138 AN INTAGLIO ON AN OVAL CONVEX QUARTZ. Cupid propping up, with some 'effort, a huge cornucopia : an inscribed gem, with the name ΑΥΛΟΥ engraved in delicate letters on one side of it

139 CUPID ; AN INTAGLIO ENGRAVED ON AN AMETHYST. The drawing and the execution are admirable

140 AN INTAGLIO, ON A FINE SARD. Cupid running under the burden of a huge mask. An excellent work of the best Roman period

An Arundel gem (Cat. Thec. A, No. 53)

141 A SMALL INTAGLIO, representing Cupid asleep on rocks, a butterfly in the field under his hand ; perhaps typifying Death. It is a good Roman work, on a pale sapphirine chalcedony

142 CUPID SINGEING A BUTTERFLY'S WINGS. A small Roman intaglio on a hyacinthine garnet

One of the Chesterfield gems in the Bessborough Collection (Cat. No. 73)

143 A CAMEO, IN THE BOLDEST RELIEF, cut in a pebble of bluish-grey translucent chalcedony. It is a head of Cupid ; the hair characteristically plaited up the centre. The work is good, and probably represents the portrait of an infant in the character of Cupid during the time of the early Empire. It is an inch and a quarter in length

One of the Medina portion of the Bessborough Collection (Cat. No. 31 M)

144 A CAMEO, ON AN ALMANDINE GARNET. A head of Cupid
A Bessborough gem (Cat. No. 86)

145 AN ANTIQUE CAMEO HEAD OF A CHILD, in high relief. It is of
fine work, on a variety of chalcedony, of a pale bluish-white,
endowed with a slight chatoyance, something like that of
moonstone. The Renaissance mounting is very pretty, consisting of "a pair of folded wings in enamelled gold, and
an elegant openwork border," with a pearl under the chin.
See Illustration, p. 101

146 AN INTAGLIO ON A SARD, of Roman work. Cupid riding on a
hippocampus
A Medina gem, No. 20 M *of Natter's Bessborough Catalogue*

147 CUPID DRIVING A PAIR OF HORSES IN A BIGA : running on
palm branch. Roman work, cut in the transparent yellowish
layer of an onyx, with a white under layer
A Bessborough gem (Cat. No. 74), *described by Natter,
possibly correctly, as a Victory*

148 TWO CUPIDS IN A SHIP : a small intaglio, on a lovely amethyst
From the Nuncio Molinari's Collection

149 AN INTAGLIO ON CORNELIAN. Two Cupids riding a boar, one
rides and whips, while another teases the animal
From the Nuncio Molinari's Collection

150 AN EXTRAORDINARILY BEAUTIFUL LITTLE CAMEO, on a five-
layered sardonyx. Cupid on a marine pard. The little
deity is cut in a layer of yellowish flesh colour ; the monster
shows a brownish-yellow tail and whitish body, relieved by a
flesh-white ground. This exquisite little gem is undoubtedly
antique, and probably belongs to the age of Hadrian, in
which the polychrome qualities of these many-layered
onyxes were much called into play

151 A CAMEO, representing Cupid in a boat drawn by dolphins. The treatment of the water is antique in its character, and the gem is probably by a Roman hand. It is cut on an onyx. In gold ring, the bezel set with rose diamonds

152 A FRAGMENT OF AN ANCIENT CAMEO, too fragmentary for the entire subject to be explained. A Cupid flying in the air, carries on a stick an object in the form of a parasol. A second Cupid, seated on the ground, apparently plays a lyre, and a third holds in his hand a (rhipis) fan in the form of an ivy-leaf. It is possible that it may have formed part of a design representing Hercules crowned by Cupids, or, as suggested by Natter, an androgynous Venus attended by Cupids : it is probably a work of the second century. The figures are cut in a white surface layer, on a base of transparent chalcedony

A Bessborough gem (Cat. No. 50)

153 A PRETTY LITTLE SARDONYX CAMEO. Cupid rendered in a white surface layer, with a swan in a brown layer, set off by a white stratum as background. The relief is extremely low, and probably belongs to the time of the Middle Empire

154 CUPID WITH HIS FOOT IN A TRAP. A small cameo on an onyx
A Bessborough gem (Cat. No. 71)

155 A SARDONYX CAMEO. Cupid sitting on the ground and playing the lyre. An admirable design, in a yellowish-white surface layer on a black ground. The drawing and the work, which is in rather low relief, are in the style of the second century
An Arundel gem (Cat. Thec. A, 138)

156 A CURIOUS LITTLE ROMAN CAMEO ; whereon four Cupids, rendered in a white upper layer, are ranged on a grey translucent under layer of a convex onyx. One plays the Pan pipes, one a flute, a third the lyre, and the fourth, a merry little figure, claps his hand and sways his foot to the movement of the music
An Arundel gem (Cat. Thec. A, 139)

157 A CAMEO, with two Cupids erecting a trophy ; of admirable
design, and probably of early Roman date
An Arundel gem (Cat. Thec. A, 137)
Figured in the " Marlborough Gems," vol. ii. 41

158 TWO CUPIDS STRUGGLING FOR A PALM BRANCH. A vigorous
little cameo, which is antique

159 THREE CUPIDS DISPORTING THEMSELVES WITH TWO DOLPHINS
IN THE WATER. An exquisite cameo, cut in the white layer of
an onyx. The figures, which are admirably finished, are in a
white layer on a black base. The mount is a broad pierced
border of enamelled gold. Microscopic figures of a Triton.
a Nereid and Cupids, with Hippocamps exquisitely carved
and enamelled, are in complete relief, while four table rubies
divide the quadrants of this most beautiful jewel ; the back is
also enamelled with scrolls, &c. in white, upon a blue translucent ground ; a work no doubt of a great Italian master in
the cinque-cento time
This gem was an acquisition of the third Duke's
See Illustration, p. 39

160 THE RENOWNED CAMEO REPRESENTING THE
HYMENEAL PROCESSION OF EROS AND PSYCHE.
The two child-like little divinities walk side by side, veiled.
even their faces being covered by the veil ; while the boy-
bridegroom presses a dove to his bosom. A winged Hymen
conducts them by a knotted cord (intended for the Cingulum,
or for the Nodus Herculis ?) ; another winged Erotic figure
prepares the nuptial couch, while over their heads the mystic
basket is borne by Anteros, conspicuous with crisply curled
wings. In the field the inscription ΤΡΥΦΩΝ ΕΠΟΙΕΙ.

The history of the gem has been so far traced that a drawing of the subject by the hand of Pirro Ligorio, early in the
16th century, was among the papers of Bagaris, as recorded
by Spon. The gem itself, which has all the characters of a
design drawn in an age of proof prints and luxurious margins,
must, moreover, have been Lord Arundel's property early in
the 17th century. In point of *technique*, it has never been

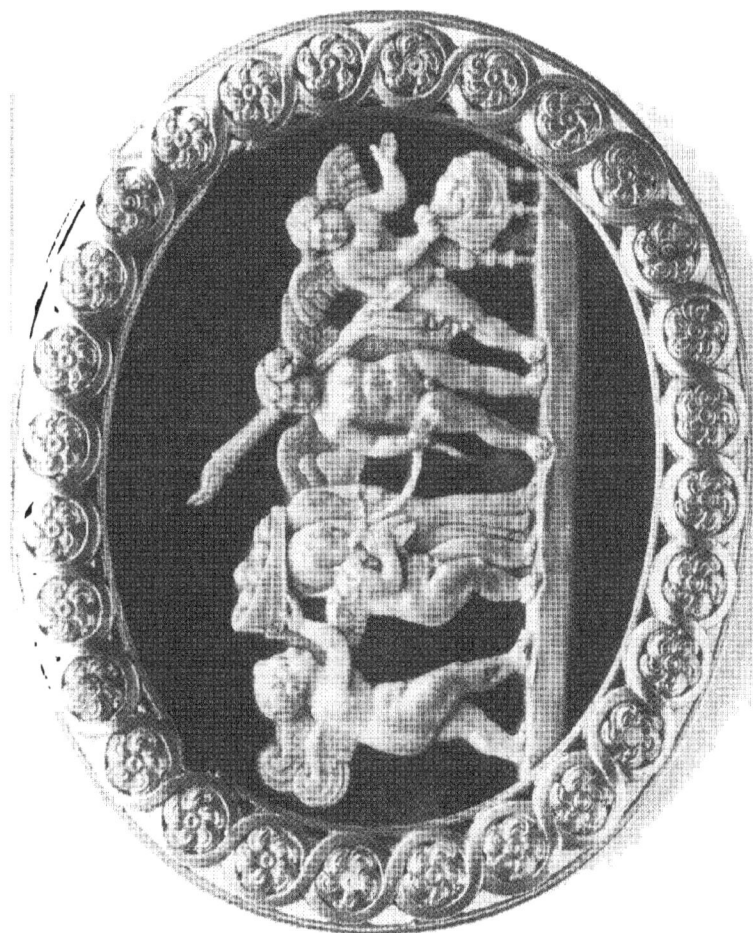

surpassed in any age. Indeed, alike for movement, for grace
of form, for tenderness of treatment and precision of modelling, as for the delicate technical management of surface,
this cameo may challenge any work of ancient or modern
times. Furthermore, the tints of the sardonyx on which it
is cut serve to typify the nocturnal purpose of the design:
the figures being rendered in a dusky layer of a pale coffee-
brown hue, seem to reflect the illuminating glare of the
torch, while the ground is of blackest sard, dark as the night
through which the half-lit figures seem moving. In gold
border set in no openwork frame, mounted with eight large
jacinths. *See Illustration*

Arundel Catalogue (Theo. II, No. :)

*Figured in the " Marlborough Gems," and by Tassie and by
Stosch, and the design has been reproduced in all sorts and
material of art, perhaps oftener than any other similar subject*

161 PSYCHE, A VEILED FIGURE, WITH A BUTTERFLY ON HER BOSOM;
her arm and fingers are just sketched in slight drawing. An
intaglio on a yellowish cornelian, perhaps of the period of
the Middle Empire. The head is to the right

162 CUPID AND PSYCHE IN PROCESSION. Intaglio on a sard; very
pretty work

*One of the Chesterfield gems (Bessborough Catalogue No.
41 c)*

163 THE GRACES; a group, with Cupid hovering in the air An
intaglio on a convex garnet, rather deeply cut and extremely
good work. The character of the engraving in this gem
corresponds with that of the antique work usual on the
garnet, and it and the design point to a Roman artist as its
author

A Chesterfield gem (Cat. No. 29 c)

154 ADONIS; an intaglio on a beautiful pale sard. In field KOIMOY
From Lord Bessborough's Collection (Cat. No. 98)

Hermes—Mercury.

165 A NOBLE GREEK INTAGLIO ON A SARD. Hermes walking plays the lyre. The figure, that of an ephebus clothed in the chlamys, the petasus hanging from his shoulder, combines the simple grace, the serenity, and the dignity of Greek design with the exquisite finish and modelling that characterise the Greek workmanship of the best period of Helladic art. It can hardly be of a later date than the 3rd century B.C.

It is figured by Worlidge (No. 6 of his Etchings) as an Apollo

166 A COPY OF No. 165 UPON AN AMETHYST. An exquisite production, in all probability one of two copies stated by Raspe to be by the hand of Burch, sen. He terms the stone a "beryl," probably by a mistake that might naturally arise from his description having been made from casts. The fidelity of the copy to the original renders it a marvel of the engraver's art. It requires much scrutiny to discriminate between the impressions taken from the two gems

167 AN INTAGLIO ON A YELLOW SARD, representing Mercury in front-faced figure. Clothed in chlamys and petasus, he holds in his hand the caduceus. The gem is figured and described by Stosch. It was once his property, but he sold it to Lord Holderness, the father-in-law of the Duke of Leeds. who, as a note in the MS. catalogue tells us, bequeathed it to the Duke of Marlborough. Its history has been traced back as far as 1589, when it was described by Montjosieu, in his "Gallus Romæ Hospes," and belonged to Tigrini. Spon described it as formerly in the hands of Fulvius Ursinus

The figure is deeply cut. The gem is inscribed with the name ΔΙΟCΚΟΥΡΙΔΟΥ. The lettering is large yet rather delicately cut

168 INTAGLIO ON A PALE YELLOW SARD, Hermes Criophorus as god
of herds ; with similar signature
A Bessborough gem (Cat. No. 102)

169 MERCURY CONVEYING THE INFANT BACCHUS TO THE NYMPHS OF
NYSA. It is very beautiful work on a jasper belonging to
the Roman time. The figure is slight and graceful, and in
a running attitude

170 MERCURY CRIOPHORUS, RESTING AGAINST A CIPPUS ; a rather
small intaglio in a cornelian. Very good Roman work

171 A LITTLE FIGURE OF MERCURY WITH HIS CADUCEUS, cock and
a tree in the field. The reverse of this gem is engraved with
another intaglio representing Venus holding scales, at her
feet Cupid, bow and quiver, in the field symbols of Libra,
Venus, Jupiter, and Mercury

172 A MERCURY ; a pretty little intaglio, on a rich hyacinthine sard.
The god leans on a column, holding the caduceus and his
emblematic purse. A cock on the ground by his side. The
astrological sign Scorpio is in the field. Probably an astrological gem embodying a fortunate horoscope. Early Roman
work.

173 MERCURY STANDING, with similar attributes to the last—the crab
on an altar representing Cancer, and like the last probably
representing a favourable horoscope of " Mercury in Cancer."
A fine intaglio, well worked, on a blood-red sard ; belonging
to the Roman period
*An Arundel gem (Cat. Thec. A, No. 51), figured in the
"Marlborough Gems," vol. i. 36, and by Worlidge in his
Etchings (No. 28)*

D

174 A STRIKING LITTLE GEM, representing the image of Mercury at the end of the perspective of a temple, which consequently projects on the stone. It is cut on a sardonyx of three layers, the image and inner end of the temple being rendered in a surface layer of brown; the five columns on either side of the temple are wrought in a white layer upon a translucent base of chalcedony, in which are four steps leading up to the temple

A Bessborough gem (Cat. No. 59); *it is figured in the " Marlborough Gems," vol. ii.* 38

175 INTAGLIO HEADS OF MERCURY AND HERCULES CONFRONTED, ON CORNELIAN. Probably an athlete's ring

An Arundel gem (Cat. Thec. A, 82)

176 A BEAUTIFUL EARLY ROMAN INTAGLIO ON A VERY FINE LAPIS LAZULI. Mercury presenting a purse to Herse, or perhaps to Fortuna

An Arundel gem (Cat. Thec. A, No. 52)

177 A CAMEO OF SLIGHTLY OVAL FORM, of rather fine and very elaborate workmanship on a singular sardonyx. The gods, as if in council, on a hemisphere representing Olympus. Jove in the centre, Neptune and Diana on one side, Venus with her Cupids and Mars on the other, behind her Mercury, and in the centre Apollo, who plays his lyre. The figures are in a white layer with a chalcedony background, while the globe is represented by a black portion of the stone

End of First Day's Sale.

Second Day's Sale.

On TUESDAY, JUNE 27, 1899,

AT ONE O'CLOCK PRECISELY.

(2.) *MINOR DIVINITIES.*

Dionysos—Bacchus.

178 A GOOD ANTIQUE WORK IN INTAGLIO ON A RED SARD. A Term
of the bearded Bacchus
From the Bessborough Collection (Cat. No. 54)

179 AN INTAGLIO ON CORNELIAN ; a head of the bearded Bacchus to
the left
A Bessborough gem (Cat. 72), called a Plato

180 BACCHUS IN FRONT FACE. An early Imperial intaglio, cut
through a white surface layer into a fine sard, which forms
the mass of the stone, which is a nicolo
*One of the gems from Lord Chesterfield's Collection (Cat.
No. 43 M)*

181 BACCHUS, a full-length figure of Roman work on a sard
*A Chesterfield gem (Cat. No. 37 c), termed by Natter "Une
Bacchante"*

182 AN INTAGLIO ON A BURNT SARD, representing a Bacchus seated
and holding out a cantharus. The face of his Pard is seen
at his knee. A large guilloche border runs round the gem
Set in silver as a seal
An Arundel gem (Cat. Thec. A, No. 85)

D 2

183 AN EXQUISITE LITTLE INTAGLIO ON A BERYL ; a full-faced figure
of Bacchus standing leaning on the thyrsus, and holding out
a cantharus. It is in high relief, and beautiful as well in finish
as in drawing: the work of doubtless a Greek artist

> An Arundel gem (Cat. Thec. A, No. 49); figured in the
> " Marlborough Gems,' vol. i. No. 33

184 A SINGULAR GEM, being a figure represented in relief in gold
appliqué on iron; it would seem to be a Bacchus, carrying a
bunch of grapes on the shoulder

185 A BEAUTIFUL CAMEO ON A SARDONYX ; probably a portrait in
the character of Bacchus. It is a profile head to the left,
with long hair, crowned with ivy leaves. The ornament of
the hair is reserved in a brown stratum, the features are in
one of bluish-white, the background being formed of a layer
of sard. The interior of the stone has been perforated along
its length : it was once doubtless strung with a set of Indian
beads. The work is probably by an artist of the reign of
Hadrian. It is s 1¾ in. high by 1½ in. in width ; in gold border
with loop

> An Arundel gem (Cat. Thec. C, 3), named a Berenice
> See Illustration, p. 66

186 AN ONYX CAMEO : Bacchus riding a panther and carrying the
thyrsus ; the figures are represented in a white layer on a
violet-grey ground. The work is probably Roman of the
3rd century

Associations, &c., of Bacchus.

187 INTAGLIO DEEPLY ENGRAVED IN A FINE SARD, representing the
front-faced figures of the youthful Bacchus with Ariadne, a
Cupid's head below, and the fragmentary face of a second and
the head of a dolphin. All the figures are supported on the
waves. The signature YΛΛΠΥ is seen in an open part of
the gem that seems as though left for it

> The gem appears to have been one of those collected by the
> third Duke, and is figured in the " Marlborough Gems," vol. i.
> No. 40

188 A FINE INTAGLIO OF A HEAD TO THE LEFT OF ARIADNE, ivy-crowned; engraved on a sard. Beautiful Greek-like drawing

An Arundel gem (Cat. Thec. A, No. 9)

189 THE SAME SUBJECT, the head to the loft, also on a sard; but the design and treatment is rather that of a good Roman artist

An Arundel gem (Cat. Thec. A, No. 81)

190 A REMARKABLE SARDONYX WITH AN INTAGLIO WORK, a sacrifice to a bearded Bacchus. The stone is oval in form, and of the dimensions of $2\frac{3}{4}$ inches long by $1\frac{3}{4}$ inch broad. It is drilled from end to end, in imitation of the Oriental agates and onyxes. The uppermost layer is of a rich brown-red, the next is bluish-white, of the kind that forms the surface of the nicolo, the lowest stratum is black. It is exceedingly beautiful, as well for its colours as for the evenness of its strata. In gold frame with loop

From Lord Bessborough's Collection (Cat. No. 17)

191 A VERY LARGE INTAGLIO ON AN AGATE. It represents Ariadne deserted by Theseus, whose ships are pushing off from the shore : Bacchus is approaching, drawn by Satyrs

An Arundel gem (Cat. Thec. E, No. 18)

192 A LARGE AND LOVELY INTAGLIO ON A SARD, representing the bust to the right of Ariadne, or of a Bacchante, crowned with ivy : Greek or Greco-Roman work. It is set in a row of turquoises, and the back is ornamented with enamel work of coloured flowers on a white ground, *temp.* Louis XIII., similar to those which adorn so many of the gems of the Arundel Collection

193 A PASTE CAMEO OF A BACCHUS AND ARIADNE

194 A MOST BEAUTIFUL CAMEO ON A SARDONYX, $1\frac{3}{4}$ inch by $1\frac{1}{4}$ inch ; Ariadne, or a Bacchante, with a wreath of ivy in her hair. This and the hair are rendered in the rich chestnut-brown upper layer, the face and neck in a porcelain-like white layer resting on a bluish-grey ground. A delicately worked gem in rather high relief, and of grand design

An Arundel gem (Cat. Thec. C, No. 4), termed Dea Libera

195 A SARDONYX CAMEO : Ariadne's or a Bacchante's head, to the
left, perhaps Faustina the younger in one of these Bacchanal
characters, with a spray of ivy in her hair. The ivy spray
is wrought in a brown layer. The shoulders are clothed
with the roe's skin, tied by the feet in front, and rendered
in high relief in a surface layer of an amber colour. The
features are given in a white stratum of this beautiful four-
layered sardonyx. It is 1⅛ inch in length by ⅞ths; in silver-
gilt setting mounted with rubies and turquoises

A Medina gem (Bessborough Cat. No. 30 M)

Figured in the 'Marlborough Gems,' vol. i. No. 31

196 A BUST PORTRAIT, to the left, in the character of Ariadne. A
noble cameo in very flat relief, on a beautiful sardonyx.
The treatment of the eye and nostril is peculiar and rude.
The features are thoughtful and evidently characteristic, and
the hair is carefully but not very delicately wrought. These,
with the neck, are rendered in a white layer of the stone,
relieved by a brown sard background ; the ivy garland, with
corymbus forming its frontlet, and the robe with its clasp,
are rendered in a surface stratum of yellow. A reserved rim
surrounds the gem, which is bevelled off on the outer side
so as to exhibit the beauty and evenness of the strata. It
seems to be a Roman work, dating perhaps from the 2nd
century ; it is 1⅛ by 1½ inch

An Arundel gem (Cat. Thec. C, No. 1), Agrippina

197 A SMALL CAMEO HEAD, to the right, of Ariadne, or of a Bacchante, on sardonyx, in high relief; the face in a white layer,
the hair in an upper layer of pale yellow, the base being also
composed of yellow sard. It is good work, and may belong
to the early Antonine period.

198 A CAMEO ON SARDONYX, being a well-wrought bust portrait to
left as Ariadne, with grapes and vine-leaves in her hair.
The hair is partially, the vine garland and robe entirely,
worked in a rich brown layer. The grapes on the garland,
and a button on the robe, are left in a white surface stratum,
while the features, hair and neck are also represented in
a lower white layer; the groundwork of the whole being a
stratum of rich brown hue. In gold frame with enamel border

199 A HEAD, to the right, in cameo, of the same favourite subject, on
a fine sardonyx. The ivy wreath and hair are rendered in a
brown, the features and throat in an opaque white layer.
The ground is of a reddish brown. The design is somewhat
undercut, and in very high relief

A Bessborough gem (Cat. No. 9)

200 A LITTLE CAMEO, representing a sacrifice to the Bearded Bacchus
by four Cupids. One of them holds a goat, one crowns a
large goblet on the ground, a third beats a tambourine, and
the fourth sings ; a statue of the Bearded Bacchus in the
centre. A minute and carefully finished work

An Arundel gem (Thec. A, No. 145)

201 A LARGE SHELL CAMEO, of fine Renaissance work, representing
a procession of Bacchus. The design and grouping of the
multitudinous figures is as skilful as the execution of them
is minute, exact, and spirited. There are no less than thirty-
three figures, including two oxen that draw the car of Bacchus,
and a lion that marches at its wheel. Thirty revellers are
thus depicted on a convex shell of 2 inches in length and
1¼ inch in width

It was an Arundel gem (Cat. Thec. D, No. 12)

202 INTAGLIO ON A BANDED AGATE. A drunken Silenus, in an
Etruscan border. He holds a thyrsus. It is ancient, and
perhaps Etruscan work

203 AN INTAGLIO OF ROMAN WORK, ON A FINE LITTLE SARD. A
drunken Silenus carrying a cantharus in his hand, and what
may be a palm branch over his shoulder

A Medina gem (No. 3 M, in the Bessborough Catalogue)

204 A STOOPING SILENUS LOOKING DOWN, WHILE A YOUNG SATYR
POURS A LIBATION OVER HIS FEET. Leaning on the right
hand of the Silenus is a thyrsus, and the Satyr carries a cloth
in his right hand. The design is enclosed in an Etruscan
border, and cut with fine skill and finish on a black sard,
deep red by transmitted light. The work has the character
of that by a good Roman artist

205 A SILENUS PROCESSION. An intaglio on a cornelian

A *Bessborough gem (Cat. No.* 24)

206 A FRAGMENT OF AN EXTRAORDINARY CAMEO. A Silenus is
pushed along by a running Satyr. The design is cut out of
the ivory-white upper layer of a splendid onyx; the under
layer consisting of black sard. A fine Roman work of the
Imperial age

An Arundel gem (Cat. Thec. B, No. 48)

207 A SMALL CINQUE-CENTO CAMEO, representing a full-faced mask
of Silenus, cut on a four-layered jasper-onyx, the curved
layers of which the engraving is made ingeniously to follow.
It is cut entirely in a surface layer of pink jasper; strata of
white, bluish-grey, and again of white underlying the pink
layer

Possibly an Arundel gem (Cat. Thec. B, No. 29)

208 AN ONYX CAMEO, representing two Satyrs supporting a drunken
Silenus. It is good Roman work

209 A CAMEO, in low relief, cut in the white surface layer of an
onyx. A Satyr lifting along Silenus in a state of helpless-
ness; a Bacchante strikes the cymbals. It is a beautiful
fragment of a larger Bacchic procession, and probably a
Roman work of the early Imperial time

Satyrs.

210 INTAGLIO ON A RED SARD, representing a laughing Satyr in
full-faced bust, with a vine garland in the hair. A fine
Greek gem, fraught with merriment

From Lord Chesterfield's Collection (Bessborough Cat. No.
39 c)

211 A RATHER SHALLOW INTAGLIO, on a fine plum-coloured amethyst.
A profile to the left of a Satyr, extraordinary for vigour
and character; his brows encircled with a vine wreath

212 AN EXQUISITE LITTLE INTAGLIO, deeply cut in a minute sard. Bust of a youthful Satyr in front face; it might be Bacchus, but that the ear seems intended to represent a pointed form. The face is looking up with a somewhat rapt expression, the head being crowned with a grape garland. It is wrought with the delicate touch of the late Italo-Greek artists.

One of the Bessborough gems (Cat. No. 56)

Figured in the "Marlborough Gems," vol. ii. 13, and forming No. 8 of Worlidge's inimitable Etchings

213 HEAD OF A YOUNG SATYR ON RED JASPER

A Chesterfield gem (Bessborough Cat. No. 28 c)

214 A SPIRITED INTAGLIO, on a circular black jasper of cabochon form. It represents a Satyr, perhaps Comus or Marsyas, seated in contemplation on the nebris, his chin resting on his left hand, and his elbow supported on his knee; his legs are crossed, and between them rests his double flute. On the margin of the gem is the inscription NICOΛAC. This gem was an acquisition of the third Duke's from the Chevalier Odam, to whom it came from the Nuncio Molinari's cabinet

Figured in the " Marlborough Gems," vol. i. No. 34)

214 *a* AND *b* ARE COPIES OF THE ABOVE, in a deep small paste, probably by Tassie

215 THIS BEAUTIFUL GEM represents a Satyr garlanded with vine, raising himself on tiptoe, and squeezing a bunch of grapes with his right hand raised above his face. The juice seems to stream down into his mouth; he carries another bunch in his left hand. The splendid stone, in which this exquisite intaglio is cut, in the delicate and shallow manner of the antique Greek artist, is a cinnamon stone garnet, in the form usually given to this stone in antiquity, viz. "en cabochon." There can be little doubt that this glorious gem dates from the later period of Greek art

An Arundel gem (Cat. Thec. A, 76)

Figured in the " Marlborough Gems," vol. ii. No. 45, and in the ninth etching of Worlidge's volumes

216 A Dancing Satyr, cut in intaglio on a brownish-red jasper.
The work and the material belong to the art of the Roman
period, and the execution of the gem is good and full of spirit

217 A Similar Subject to No. 216. An intaglio, on a yellowish
backed sard

218 A Dancing Satyr; an intaglio on a cornelian. It is mounted
in a ring with a beautiful enamelled setting of thyrsi and
ivy-leaves

A Bessborough gem (Cat. No. 58)

219 A Satyr Reposing, leaning on a pillar, on which is a bust and
the roe-skin; in the field a Term supporting the Satyr's staff

From the Chesterfield Collection (Cat. No. 30 c)

220 An Onyx Cameo, representing a Satyr with his infant on his
knee. The figure rendered in a white layer on a black
ground

An Arundel gem (Cat. Thec. B, No. 45)
Figured in the " Marlborough Gems," vol. i. No. 44)

221 A Roman Intaglio, on a sard, representing a Satyr sitting in
repose, and contemplating a trophy of arms

One of the Medina gems (Bessborough Cat. No. 1 m)

222 A Satyr Pouring out a Libation before a Priapic Term.
An intaglio deeply engraved in a long oval cornelian. The
whole design is well balanced, and the figure of the Satyr
pouring from his wine-skin into the (cantharus) vase at his
right hand, as he sits at ease on a pard's skin, is very grace-
fully modelled. His pedum lies on the ground, and the
thyrsus leans against the Term; a crater is in the field
beyond. The setting is one of the series of beautiful enamel
work, tulips of exquisitely delicate workmanship, painted in
enamel on a white ground temp Louis XIII.

An Arundel gem (Cat. Thec. E, No. 10)

No. 226.

No. 37.

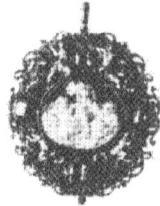

No. 159.

No. 538.

No. 478.

No. 565.

223 An Old Satyr, sitting on a pard's skin, apparently plays the double flute; an infant Satyr, holding a thyrsus, dances, while a Nymph, sitting by, waves her hand as though to mark the time. This pretty little family scene is engraved in rather deep intaglio, on an extraordinary sard of fine red colour and transparency, and the design is surrounded by a granulated border. It is doubtless by the hand of a Greek artist, probably of Magna Græcia

224 A Little Festival, wherein a seated Silenus plays the lyre, a Satyr stands and blows the double pipe, a young Satyr bestrides a pard, while from out of an overshadowing tree, which with a vine on the other side forms a sort of border to the design, a second little Satyr looks down on the scene. Cut in intaglio, on a fine yellowish sard of a peculiar quality, transmitting a greenish tint. It appears to be a Roman gem of early Imperial age

From the Medina Collection (Cat. No. 46 m)

225 Two Satyrs Playing the Tibia; a Cupid running to one of them. A rather large intaglio on a sard. One of the players sits on what appears to be a ram's skin

An Arundel gem (Cat. Thec. E, No. 21)

226 A Bacchanal Subject. A cameo, antique in character, wrought in a beautiful porcelain-white upper stratum of a sardonyx, with a yellow base layer. The moulding of the limbs and form of the Mænad in the foreground is extraordinarily delicate, and the attitudes of the remaining figures, viz. a Satyr teasing a panther, and a second Mænad, who is at hand to beat the tambourine, are artistically drawn. A reserved rim surrounds the design, which is set in an enamelled border of tulips and other flowers. The *technique* of this gem resembles the cinque-cento works, but the details betray none of the errors in archæology so characteristic of an uncritical age; and the work is therefore probably by an ancient artist of a noble school

See Illustration

227 A BACCHANTE ON A FINE RED SARD. A Renaissance intaglio
An Arundel gem (Cat. Thec. E, No. 14)

228 A VERY FINE SHALLOW INTAGLIO, of exquisite workmanship,
especially in the flowing drapery; cut on an oval somewhat convex amethyst of a beautiful tint. It represents a
Bacchante in extasy; and in the workmanship no less than
in the character of the surface it bespeaks an antique
hand, probably that of a Greek artist of the third or fourth
century B.C.

229 A SHALLOW AND DELICATE INTAGLIO, on a small almandine, cut
" en cabochon." A Nymph (possibly, however, Diana),
running, blows the flute; a hound runs by her feet. Undoubtedly a Roman work

230 A BEAUTIFULLY WROUGHT INTAGLIO, on a perfect little plasma
of the purest translucent green. A Bacchante in frenzy
clashing the cymbals, and abandoning herself to the dance
they excite. The gem must have been a work of Roman
art before its decline, and not only the drawing but the
execution is remarkably fine

231 A REPRESENTATION OF PRIAPUS WORSHIP

232 A BACCHANTE BEFORE A PRIAPIC TERM, a thyrsus in her hand.
A good Roman, rather shallow, intaglio, on a fine, clear,
yellowish sard

233 A RENAISSANCE INTAGLIO, on a beautiful tricoloured agate. It
represents a Nymph sacrificing to Priapus

234 A BACCHANAL ORGIE, with the signature ΑΛΛΙΩΝΟΣ, a Satyr
and Nymph embracing, a Priapic Term in the field, and a
Pan playing the double flute. It is an intaglio on a large
oblong beryl, and is stated by Natter to have been the work
of Flavio Sirletti. Mounted in gold as a seal with vase-
shaped stem

A Bessborough gem (Cat. No. 22)

235 AN ANTIQUE CAMEO. A Satyr and Nymph represented in the
white upper layer of a black and white jasper onyx. In
chased ring with rose diamond on each shoulder
A Medina gem (Cat. No. 25 M)

236 A SMALL RENAISSANCE CAMEO ON AN ONYX. A Nymph assailed
by a Satyr, but defended by a soldier with a drawn sword
*From the Bessborough Collection; termed by Natter (Cat.
No. 28) "L'enlèvement de Cassandre par Ajax"*

Pan.

237 A HEAD OF PAN, crowned with the vine, in full face; a very
fine intaglio. A work of Roman art
An Arundel gem (Cat. Thec. A, No. 5)

238 INTAGLIO ON A SARD. Pan returning from the chase; in one
hand he holds a plate of fruit; in the other, together with
his crook, he has the skin of a roe or a goat that he has killed.
It is a good Roman work. Mounted as a seal
An Arundel gem (Cat. Thec. A, 54)

239 A FINE UNDOUBTEDLY GREEK INTAGLIO ON A BROWN SARD.
Pan sitting, with a thyrsus leaning on his shoulder, contemplates a comic mask, which he holds in his hands. The
work is deeply engraved

240 A SPIRITED ONYX CAMEO, representing Pan erect before a
reclining figure of an aged man, both in a gesticulating
attitude, as if in argument: intended probably to embody
the idea of an author of the Satyric Drama declaiming, the
Pan being introduced to express this. The figures are
rendered in a white layer over a yellow sard ground. The
gem is probably a work of the Augustan date. It is
mounted very beautifully in an exquisite ring with masks of
Satyrs on the shoulders, a work of some cinque-cento Italian
goldsmith
*A Bessborough gem: called by Natter a river-god (Cat.
No. 101)*

(3.) PRIMEVAL GODS.

Chronos—Saturn.

241 SATURN, HIS FALX (?) IN HIS LEFT, his sceptre in his right hand.
Extremely shallow intaglio, on a singularly streaked and
' smoke-tinted chalcedony. Set as a seal

An Arundel gem, called a Jupiter (Ar. Cat. Thec. A, No. 50)

242 A HEAD OF CYBELE TO THE LEFT IN INTAGLIO, on a fine sard,
or the subject may represent a city, perhaps the portrait of
Berenice in the character of one. It is a gem of good workmanship; early Imperial, or perhaps late Greek

A Bessborough gem (Cat. No. 69)

243 A ROMAN INTAGLIO, engraved on a very fine nicolo, with its
colours beautifully contrasted. It represents Cybele crowned
with her towers, and drawn in her lion-chariot

An Arundel gem (Cat. Thec. A, No. 73)

The Fates.

244 CLOTHO WITH HER DISTAFF; a fine intaglio on a dark sard
A Bessborough gem (Cat. No. 105)

Hades—Pluto ; Persephone—Proserpine.

245 A GOOD INTAGLIO IN SARD, representing perhaps Proserpine, if
the ornament be wheat-ears over her brow, mounted in a
heavy cinque-cento ring of gold, enamelled in black with the
initials D·IЙS·B upon it. The head is to the left, and may
be a work of Hadrian's time

An Arundel gem (Cat. Thec. I, No. 8)?

246 A BEAUTIFUL SHALLOW INTAGLIO, on a blue beryl, probably a fine Sicilian Greek gem. Proserpine's head to the left is represented in profile without the wheat-ears, but dressed in the mitra. The artist's hand has worked in the shallow relief with much delicacy of touch. "A gem identical in subject and similar in treatment existed in the Praun (Mertens-Schaffhausen) Collection (No. 1080), on an antique black paste

247 A FINE INTAGLIO ON A PALE SARD WORTHY OF IT. Hades, enthroned, holds the sceptre in the right hand, a thunderbolt in the left. Persephone veiled stands before him. The gem is engraved with a bold and almost rough execution; but with much refinement of drawing, a combination rare except in Hellenic art. The drapery, done in shallow relief on the figure of Persephone, and deeply sunk on the lower limbs of the god, is very statuesque in its character

248 A SMALL ONYX CAMEO. A head to the left, perhaps a portrait, of the class, from the head-dress, usually called Persephone

(4.) *DEITIES OF DESTINY; OF HEALTH;*
TUTELARY DEITIES, &c.

249 A REPRESENTATION IN INTAGLIO, ON A SARD, of a winged figure standing on the prostrate form of a man. It is a figure of Nemesis; round it is the inscription, TO ΔШГON NYNCHN

250 FORTUNA, holding a cornucopia in the left hand, wheat-ears and the characteristic rudder in her right hand. An intaglio, cut in an effective style of art, in a rich brown surface-layer on a splendid sardonyx, the sides of which, bevelled away, exhibit the other strata of the stone, one being of a dark greyish-brown, and below it a white layer. It appears to be a Roman work

Asklepios--Æsculapius, &c.

251 A HEAD OF ÆSCULAPIUS TO THE LEFT, an intaglio on a fine yellowish-red sard, with the characteristic Zeus-like cast of feature. The serpent entwining a staff is in the field. It is a noble gem, worthy of a Greek artist

252 HYGIEA SEATED, feeds a serpent which entwines a cippus, on which is a tripod carrying a globe. An intaglio on a cornelian. Fine Roman work

253 ÆSCULAPIUS AND HYGIEA IN INTAGLIO ON A SARD
An Arundel gem (Cat. Thec. A, 55)

Cities personified, &c.

254 INTAGLIO ON A STRIPED AGATE ; a standing figure, with cornucopia in the right, and a serpent (coiled round his arm) in the left hand. The work is bold, and in character like the late Roman gems of the second century
An Arundel gem (Cat. Thec. A, 89)]

255 HEAD OF JANUS: a cameo on sardonyx, done in a yellowish-brown surface layer on a white ground. (On the back is a medley of conjugated masks)
A Bessborough gem (Cat. No. 34)

256 A VAST NICOLO, 1¾ inch long and ¾ inch high, carrying an intaglio. A central figure over which is a rude inscription, engraved directly, OYPANIA HPA seems to represent the Astarte of Libya or Carthage riding a lion, and with a sceptre in her hand. The Dioscuri, each with a star over their heads, stand, the one in advance and the other to the rear of the lion. ΑΜΜΩΝΙΟΣ ΑΝΕΘΗΚΕ ΕΠ ΑΓΑΘΩ is in the exergue—" Dedicated by Ammonios for a blessing." It is perhaps an African gem cut during the 3rd or 4th century A.D. Mounted in gold as a ring
A Bessborough gem (Cat. No. 4 M). Published by Venuti, and cited in the Corpus Inscript. No. 7034

Hebe—Juventas.

257 A SHALLOW INTAGLIO ON A BANDED' AGATE. A female, half-draped figure, drinking out of a patera ; a type which, from its occurring on coins, with the legend IUVENTAS, is entitled a Hebe. It is an antique gem carrying an Etruscan border, and probably Greek work of an early date, perhaps 400 B.C.

A Bessborough gem (Cat. No. 61)

258 A SMALL CAMEO ON A SARDONYX. In the upper bluish porcelain-like layer is a figure representing the Roman personification of youth, perhaps a Hebe. The design not unlike the preceding, being that so frequent as a half-draped figure in graceful attitude, drinking from a patera. The base stratum of the stone is of sard, and the work seems of Roman time

In catalogues of the last century this figure is designated sometimes as Semiramis, sometimes as Sophonisba, drinking the poison

259 A WINGED "HEBE," by Marchant, and signed by him. A beautiful intaglio on a yellow sard, stated to have been copied from an Etruscan bas-relief in the British Museum. The figure is beautiful and highly finished

260 AN INTAGLIO REPRESENTING, PROBABLY, A HEBE. A winged figure, cut in a red sard, pours from an œnochoe into a patera ; boldly handled by an artist of the later period of the Early Empire

A Bessborough gem (Cat. No. 75)

E

Nike—Victoria.

261 A HEAD OF VICTORY, laurel-crowned, to the left. A very fine Roman intaglio on a deep red sard

An Arundel gem (Cat. Thec. A, 80)

262 A CAMEO ON A BEAUTIFUL LITTLE SARDONYX. A wingless Victory crowns a warrior in a biga; another Victory, winged, acts as charioteer to him. It was once the property of Cardinal Albani, and is signed by the incised name ΑΛ✦ΗΟϹ. The signature occurs in the blank left under the ground on which the chariot and horses stand. The whole group, and in particular the horses, is admirably drawn and executed. The gem is cut in a porcelain-white layer, which overlies the fine brown sard that forms the foundation of the stone. The work has all the character of a Roman gem of the time of the early " Cæsars "

Figured in the " Marlborough Gems," vol. ii. No. 47

263 VICTORY WINGED, in a biga; a spirited cameo: the figures in a blackish-brown layer in relief on a white ground

It was a Medina gem (Bessborough Catalogue No. 19 M)

264 VICTORY IN A BIGA. A cameo on a sardonyx. The near horse and chariot-wheel are rendered in a black layer, the rest of the figures in a bluish-white layer, the base being formed of dark sard. The treatment of the horses and of the dress belongs to a good Roman period

An Arundel gem (Cat. Thec. D, No. 14)

(5.) *DEITIES OF TIME ; OF LIGHT, &c.*

265 A BEAUTIFUL INTAGLIO, representing a female figure moving forward in a dress fluttering behind her from her rapid movement ; a tree and a Cupid in the field. It is engraved in a Roman style of a not very late date, on a red sard. It represents the Season of the Spring

An Arundel gem (Cat. Thec. A, No. 58)

The Sun God.

266 "Solis Figura," Sol.: an intaglio on a "Venus-hair stone" (the Solis gemma of Pliny?); quartz crystal with rutile fibres in it. It is a full-length figure of Roman art. It is set in a ring elegantly enamelled with black, and with turquoise-blue dots

An Arundel gem (Cat. Thec. A, 48)

267 A Similar Subject, his whip in his hand, on a singular yellow jasper, its back being of a mottled green, whereon is engraved directly the word CEMECEIAAM. This title ("Eternal sun") has generally another application in Gnostic amulets, being usually associated with Cnoph or the Abraxas deity

An Arundel gem (Cat. Thec. A, 47)

268 An Intaglio on a Fine Nicolo. Sol in a quadriga, a trident in the field. In massive gold ring, the shoulders decorated with scale pattern

An Arundel gem (Cat. Thec. A, No. 41)

269 Sol in a Quadriga. Roman work, cut in intaglio on a sard, mounted as a seal

An Arundel gem (Cat. Thec. A, 88)

270 The Head of the Dog Sirius, radiated and open-mouthed, in front face. A very renowned intaglio, most profoundly cut, and marvellously finished in a material worthy of it, the kind of carbuncle known as the "Siriam" or "Syriam" garnet, as being obtained of the finest quality from the neighbourhood of the ancient capital of Pegu

On the collar of the dog is the signature ΓΑΙΟΣ ΕΠΟΙΕΙ. Natter first described it in his "Traité de la Méthode Antique de Graver," &c., No. XVI., and also in the Bessborough Catalogue, No. 40 c, and he acknowledges to have copied it. His copy, in topaz, is at St. Petersburg. Other gems with the subject, some of them certainly antique, but similarly treated, exist in different collections; one is in the Payne Knight Collection in the British Museum, and another in that at Berlin

E 2

Eos—Aurora.

271 AURORA IN A BIGA, clad with the arching veil of the antique
HΩΣ. It is wrought on a sardonyx in extraordinary relief
and with transcendent excellence. The near horse must
once have been carved nearly " in the round," for it almost
prances in the air. The axle of the chariot carries a
minute silver stud. The material might have been chosen
to represent the subject, the figures being carved in a most
beautiful ivory-like layer, while the background, over which
they are moving, is a yellow sard, that might express the
amber light of the opening morning

It was one of the Arundel gems (Cat. Thec. B, No. 41)

Figured in the " Marlborough Gems," vol. ii. No. 39)

272 IN THIS FINE CAMEO WE HAVE THE SAME SUBJECT VERY
SIMILARLY TREATED. In each the figure and garb of Aurora
are quite similar, and she holds the reins in her two hands in
the same way. Indeed the two gems might both have been
copies from the same original. This beautiful gem is cut in
a jasper onyx, hardly less appropriate in the accordance of
the colours of the stone with the subject represented than
the last ; the figures, carved in a wax-like layer, present a
more dusky hue, and seem emerging from the night ; the
background of the gem being formed of a layer of blackest
jasper. One can hardly assign to this gem a later date than
that of the Rome of Augustus

An Arundel gem (Cat. Thec. C, No. 21)

Figured in the " Marlborough Gems," vol. ii. No. 48

See Illustration

273 PHAETON, his chariot and horses, represented in the white layer
of an onyx ; in slight relief. In open frame setting with
amethysts, &c.

One of the Medina gems (Cat. No. 39 M)

No. 272.

No. 596.

No. 350.

No. 283.

No. 591.

No. 38.

(6.) *ASTROLOGICAL SUBJECTS OF PAGAN CHARACTER.*

274 A TRIUMPHAL CAR, surrounded by all the signs of the zodiac. A Victory holding out a wreath, floats in the air over a quadriga. The gem is finished in minute detail, and is contained in a minute sard of circular form and of a somewhat obscure yellow-brown colour, the diameter of which is but ⅗ths of an inch. Baron Roger de Sivry possesses in his collection a gem in all respects similar to this

Figured in Worlidge's Etchings, No. 39

275 A SUBJECT OF WHICH A REPRESENTATION EXISTS ON A GEM IN THE FRENCH IMPERIAL CABINET. Jove with his eagle, and with Mercury on the one hand, and Mars on the other, stands on a hemispherical frame, below which Neptune with his trident raises half his form from out of the ocean. Around the whole is a zodiac. The intaglio is cut in a large cornelian of 1¾ inch in diameter, and no doubt represents a horoscope

The mounting is an elaborate production of an Italian artist, the stone being set round with table diamonds and spinel rubies, interspersed with enamelled roses and other flowers, and suspended by a triple chain. On the back is a representation, in richly coloured enamel, of a stork-shaped imaginary bird

An Arundel gem (Cat. Thec. E, No. 11)
See Illustration, p. 101

276 AN INTAGLIO ON AN AGATE. A winged female goddess and a Cupid are in the centre; on one side a figure apparently meant for Apollo, and another playing Pan's pipes; two unrecognisable personages are on the other side

From the Bessborough Collection. It is stated by Natter (Cat. No. 23) to have been previously in the Collection of Mr. Stanhope

(7.) *MITHRAIC SUBJECTS.*

278 AN INTAGLIO ON A HÆMATITE. An amulet, very curious on
account of the combination, probably not accidental, of the
Mithraic subject on the obverse with an Abraxas on the
reverse. The former is the usual representation of Mithras
slaughtering the bull; the crab and a serpent below in the
field, besides an eagle, a jackal, two altars, and two heads.
The style far superior to that of the majority of these talis-
mans; it is no doubt a work of the second century. Mounted
in gold slide

279 A RENAISSANCE RENDERING OF THE LAST DESIGN, but it is without the proper attributes of the Mithraic subject of it, and
would be more correctly, perhaps, described as a wingless
Victory sacrificing a bull. It is an intaglio well cut on a
cornelian, and is set in a very pretty Louis XIV. seal

A Bessborough gem (Cat. No. 106)

280 A MITHRAIC SUBJECT IN INTAGLIO, on bloodstone. Perhaps the
Soul and the two Principles, and is much like the gem in
the Praun Collection, figured in p. 359 of Mr. King's work
on antique gems. A work of perhaps the first century.
Mounted as a seal

*One of the Chesterfield gems in the Bessborough Collection
(Cat. No.* 38 c)

281 A Horus Harpocrates, seated in the boat of the Sun on a lotos
flower, wearing the disc of the sun, raising his left hand to
his mouth, and holding in his right a whip; adored by a
Cynocephalus, wearing on his head a disc (sacred to the moon).
At the prow and stern a hawk, the emblem of Horus, crowned
with Pschent (the crown of the upper and lower world); in
the field the sun and moon. It is a well cut Romano-Egyptian intaglio, on a curious jasper of a dull brownish red, with
a stain of green in it

  An Arundel gem (Cat. Thec. A, No. 99)

282 Harpocrates. A full-length figure in intaglio, on a splendid red
sard. His finger on his lip (as a divinity of Silence), he
holds on his left hand a cornucopia, resting on a column. On
his head is the persea fruit. It is a fine work of Romano-
Egyptian art

283 A Seated Harpocrates, his forefinger on his lip, his left hand
holding the cornucopia. A cameo in the highest relief, cut
in a fine porcelain-white layer of a fine sardonyx, the lower
layer consisting of red-brown sard. The modelling of the
figure is delicate, and the finish of the work excellent.
Mounted as a slide for a necklet in gold, enamelled with
scroll design in black, &c. on white ground

  An Arundel gem (Cat. Thec. B, No. 43)
  See Illustration, p. 48

284 A Very Fine Copy, probably by Natter, of the Sphinx of
Thamyras, in the Blacas Collection. It is an intaglio on a
most magnificent sard

  A Bessborough gem (Cat. No. 92)

* For Isis, see under Demeter, Nos. 43 to 46; and for Serapis, see under
Zeus, Nos. 5 to 11.

285 A CANOPIC VASE ; a head rising from it, covered with the head-dress of Osiris. Probably, on this account, of Roman time, as the Egyptian representation of this subject has the heads of four divinities in place of the Osiris head. Such vases appear to have been used to contain the intestines of the deceased. The intaglio is cut in the brown upper layer of a convex sardonyx, with an underlayer of white. An inscription ΦΙΛΙΠ ΠΟΥ, doubtless the owner's name, surrounds the vase, on which arabesque-looking ornaments are seen. The work is ancient, and is probably a work of late Romano-Egyptian art

An Arundel gem (Cat. Thec. A, No. 83)

286 THE SAME SUBJECT, finely engraved on a cinnamon stone of great beauty. The vase has hieroglyphics on it. Its date is probably coeval with the last

290 AN AMULET WITH THREE K's, with a Coptic inscription in direct Greek characters, ΘΩΒΑΡΡΑΒΑΥΔΡΥΩΣΣ. A Gnostic work of the fourth century ; at the back Hercules strangling a lion, intaglio in red jasper. This amulet is that prescribed by Alexander of Trallos, as a charm against the colic

An Arundel gem (Cat. Thec. A, No. 87). This gem was once in the Collection of Gorlæus (see No. 441 Gorlæi Dactylotheca), afterwards purchased by King James I. for his son

Section II.—THE HEROES.

(1.) *HERACLEAN CYCLE.*

291 A FRAGMENT OF A HEAD OF HERCULES, to the left, very skilfully made up in gold: it is a very deep intaglio, of the " Glycon " type, and perhaps of Greek work, in a most simple and grand style, in a cornelian, and was once a gem of large size. In enamelled mount

An Arundel gem (Cat. Thee. E, No. 29)

292 A HEAD OF HERCULES, to the left, of Roman work, on a burnt sard. Set in gold as a seal

Figured No. 20 of Worlidge's Etchings

293 INTAGLIO ON A GOOD SARD. The same subject to the left; a wreath, probably meant for poplar, on the head. It may be a portrait of a late emperor, perhaps of Maximian, as Hercules

An Arundel gem (Cat. Thec. A, No. 38)

294 HEAD OF THE YOUTHFUL HERCULES, to the left: an intaglio on a fine sard

A Bessborough gem, Chesterfield portion (Cat. No. 13 c)

295 HERCULES MINGENS, Roman work, in intaglio, on a greyish-coloured agate

296 THE CELEBRATED HERCULES BIBAX, with the lettering ΑΔΜΩΝ behind the figure, which is a full-length side figure to the left carrying a vast club. The signature, which seems ancient, and fills a place evidently left for it in the design, would be limited by the form of the ω to the Roman Period. Indeed, the heaviness of the figure belongs to a time much later than even the original of the Farnese Hercules; the early athletic type of Hercules degenerating into more massive and clumsy exaggerations as we trace it down from the older Greek to the later Roman artists. It may even be a work of Caracalla's time.

This fine gem is cut in not very deep intaglio on a slightly convex sard; the lettering, besides being in the nominative, is too large to be the signature of the artist, and no doubt, as Dr. Brunn supposes, represents the name of the owner. A gem with this design (figured by Stosch) belonged to the Collection of Vitelleschi Verospi; another figured by Worlidge (in 1768), (No. 21) was this, of the Marlborough Collection. Bracci and Visconti speak of such a gem as in the Nuncio Molinari's Collection, a statement considered by Dr. Brunn to militate against the Marlborough gem being that of the Verospi cabinet. Raspe, however, states that this gem came to the Duke of Marlborough's Collection from that of Molinari, into which it had passed, he says, from the Verospi Cabinet.

A careful comparison of this gem and that in the Blacas Collection shows this to be the finer and more antique looking work.

Figured in the "Marlborough Gems," vol. i. No. 32

297 A FULL-LENGTH FRONT FIGURE OF THE YOUTHFUL HERCULES, with the hide of the lion on one arm, the club in the hand of the other. A most excellent intaglio, of the best period of Roman work, on a superb red sard, perfect as well in its transparency as in its colour

298 HERCULES REPOSING : the subject of the Colossus at Tarentum,
brought to Rome by Fabius, and originally executed by
Lysippus. Other copies exist with the motto, ΠΟΝΟΣ ΤΟΥ
ΚΑΛΩΣ ΗΣΥΧΑΖΕΙΝ ΑΙΤΙΟΣ. One was in the Orleans
Collection

An Arundel gem (Cat. Thec. E, 13)

299 THE SAME SUBJECT, on what looks like an antique stone, a red
sard

300 AN INTAGLIO OF THE SAME SUBJECT, on a white cornelian

301 A ROMAN INTAGLIO, representing Hercules wrestling with
Antæus, on a fine little lapis lazuli, somewhat convex. It
is mounted in a beautiful ring, with a white enamelled
fleur-de-lis, and black arabesque work of entwined vines

An Arundel gem (Cat. Thec. Δ, 56)

303 HERCULES SUPPORTING ANTIOPE, the dying Queen of the
Amazons : paste, imitating a deep red sard

304 INTAGLIO ON A MAGNIFICENT DARK SARD. Hercules having
brought back Alcestis from the shades, presents her to her
astonished husband. This is perhaps the chef-d'œuvre of
Marchant, and exhibits the excellencies of his style. The
graceful form of the wife stands in contrast with the erect
demi-god, who, raising the veil of Alcestis, gives her back
to Admetus. In the exergue N.MARCHANT INV.ET.F. The
figure of Admetus is more feeble in design, and the proportion of the head is in each figure too small. But though
with little of the austere spirit of antique art, the conception
of the gem is good, recalling somewhat the motive of the
gem numbered 9211 in Tassie ; the heralds leading off Briseis.
Work so finished was impossible, except in an age supplied
with lenses of high power. This fine gem was a present
from the Elector Duke of Saxony, in return for a copy of
the " Marlborough Gems," presented to his Serene Highness
by the third Duke of Marlborough. On the back of the gem
an inscription in beautifully cut letters " Saxoniæ Princeps
doni memor," commemorates the occasion of so princely a
gift

305 HEAD OF HERCULES, in full face. A cameo in hyacinthine garnet

306 A CAMEO CUT IN A WHITE LAYER WITH A DARK GROUND. Hercules bibax, with Lilliputian Cupids

An Arundel gem (Cat. Thec. D, No. 16)

307 HERCULES. A minute modern cameo, the letters HPAK in the field : in a bluish-white layer on a black base

308 HERCULES STRANGLING THE LION; a large cameo on an onyx. A very spirited antique work

Figured in the " Marlborough Gems," vol. ii. No. 44

309 AN ANTIQUE CAMEO, representing a bust to the right of Om-phale ; in design similar to No. 313. Cut in a double nicolo, of indubitable antiquity, having the original Indian perforation traversing it. At the back is a full-faced cameo bust of Hercules, of Renaissance work. It has been worked in order to take advantage of the fine bluish film at the back of this very extraordinary *double* nicolo. This gem possesses an historical interest, from its having been presented by Charles V. to Pope Clement VII., and by him subsequently to the Piccolomini of Sienna. It is mounted in a broad gold setting with eight table diamonds and rubies, alternately, on either face ; and between each pair of these stones is a delicate filigree ornament of triplets of trefoil, tied into a sort of golden fleur-de-lis. The edge is ornamented with a twist of vine branches and leaves in black enamel. The setting is of the same period as the gift

A Medina gem (Cat. No. 28 M.)

Figured by Borioni in the " Museum Piccolomini," Pl. III. (No. 45)

Also in the " Marlborough Gems," vol. ii. No. 18

See Illustration

No. 103.

No. 103.

No. 309.

No. 309.

310 A CAMEO, of Renaissance workmanship, the subject being similar
to that of No. 295

An Arundel gem (Cat. Thec. A, No. 142)

311 A HEAD TO THE LEFT OF THE YOUTHFUL HERCULES, with the
lion's skin head-dress. It is an intaglio of the most beautiful
workmanship and of the purest design, engraved by a Greek
artist of the best period on a fine golden sard

Once Lord Chesterfield's (Bessborough Cat. No. 6 c)

312 A HEAD OF OMPHALE, to the left (or Iole?), in the garb of
Hercules, with the lion's skin head-dress ; below, ΓΝΑΙΟC.
It is beautifully finished, and is cut in a orange sard of the
finest colour and quality ·

A Bessborough gem (Cat. No. 43)

313 THE SAME SUBJECT, in profile to the left, on a fine hyacinthine
sard

*Once Lord Chesterfield's. A Bessborough gem (Cat.
No. 14 c)*

314 A FULL-LENGTH INTAGLIO OF OMPHALE, in the Herculean lion's-
skin garb, semi-nude. A beautifully modelled and finished
gem, of good Greek work, on a somewhat convex pale
amethyst

*One of the Medina gems in Lord Bessborough's Collection
(Cat. No. 7 M)*

*Figured in the " Marlborough Gems," vol. ii. No. 46, and
among Worlidge's Etchings, No. 40*

315 THE SAME SUBJECT, in intaglio on a golden sard, by a Greek engraver

317 OMPHALE, profile to the right, same subject as those previously described. It is a cameo in the style of the third century; the hair is worked in a yellowish surface layer, the face in a stratum of opaque white on a ground of bluish black

An Arundel gem (Cat. Thec. B, No. 20)

318 THE SAME SUBJECT TO THE LEFT; a work in cameo, on an onyx of a singular quality and colour

An Arundel gem (Cat. Thec. B, No. 17)

319 A REMARKABLE CAMEO IN LAPIS LAZULI, representing profile busts to the right of Hercules and Iole, or rather portraits so personified. The appearance of the gem is antique, and especially Græco-Egyptian; the eyes in particular, from their somewhat staring expression, and the line round the iris, seem to indicate this. The portraits may possibly be those of a Ptolemy and his queen, or they may represent personages of importance during the reign of a Ptolemy

An Arundel gem (Cat. Thec. C, No. 9)

Leander.

320 INTAGLIO HEAD, to the left, of Leander or the figure called in
catalogues Leucothoe (a moon behind the head). Cut in a
bold style of Roman workmanship, in a circular red sard
A Bessborough gem (Cat. No. 42)

321 HERO AND LEANDER, intaglio. A work on a very fine sard (a
sardine), its age being sufficiently indicated by the representation of the Winds
A Bessborough gem (Cat. No. 85)

322 LEANDER. A bust to the left, as though swimming, cut in intaglio
on a sard ; perhaps of Roman work
*An Arundel gem (Cat. Thee. A, No. 28), termed "Caput
Athletæ"*

Meleager.

323 A VERY FINE SARD, with a figure of a huntsman carrying a spear,
probably Meleager ; cut in intaglio, in a somewhat slight
manner : an antique work
A Bessborough gem, termed Adonis (Cat. No. 32 c)

324 A WORK IN INTAGLIO, on a sard, called by Nattor, in his Catalogue of the Bessborough Gems, a "Meleager"
(Bess. Cat. No. 97)

325 A BEAUTIFUL BIT OF MINUTE ITALIAN RENAISSANCE WORK,
comprising 27 figures, and styled "The Death of Meleager."
It is cut in shallow cameo on the top of a shell of Cyprœa
tigris
An Arundel gem (Cat. Thee. C, No. 18)

Amazons.

326 A CAMEO OF RARE BEAUTY, and in the finest antique work. An
Amazon, whose helmet is cut in a little boss of transparent red
sard, supports her dead comrade, whose horse stands by looking towards the distant conflict. The figures are cut out of
an ivory-white layer upon a fine brownish sard base
Figured in the " Marlborough Gems," vol. i. No. 48

327 A CAMEO, representing an Amazon unhorsed, and seized by a
warrior (Theseus and Antiope). The stone is a sardonyx, so
cut that the Amazon is represented in a surface layer of opaque
white, the horse and the warrior in a hornlike stratum, on a
base of chalcedony. The work belongs to the best Roman
period

Bellerophon and Pegasus.

328 BELLEROPHON AND PEGASUS, a chimæra below; a Roman intaglio
engraved on a nicolo
An Arundel gem (Cat. Thec. A, No. 64)

329 BELLEROPHON WATERING PEGASUS AT THE HIPPOCRENE. Inscribed
VOTAI. An intaglio cut in a rich shaded sard

[Pegasus.]

330 THE FORE QUARTERS AND WING OF PEGASUS, beautifully engraved in intaglio in a hyacinth. The curl of the wing is in
the most authentically antique manner, like that on coins of
Lampsacus, or of Corinth

Theseus.

331 THESEUS, having slain the Minotaur, rests on his club; the dead
monster lies in a window of the Labyrinth; a very pretty
cameo cut in a porcelain-white layer in relief, on a bluish-
grey base

Heroes of the Trojan War.

332 PRIAM AT THE FEET OF ACHILLES. A beautiful little Greek intaglio on a fine sard. Four figures are included in the design, of which the finish is complete, even to the ornamentation of the cuirass of Achilles

> *One of the Medina gems (Bessb. Cat. No. 44 M)*

333 A SEATED WARRIOR, in intaglio (called in the Blenheim Catalogue an Achilles), contemplates a helmet. It is engraved on a beautiful little sard

334 AN INTAGLIO; a crouching warrior (the so-called wounded Achilles—perhaps Tydeus); a round buckler covers his side with a Gorgon head on it, and his sword is erect in his hand before him. It is cut deeply into a good pale sard in an antique style

335 A CAMEO, Roman in date, on sardonyx. Achilles or a hero holding forth a sword. He is seated on a cuirass. It is cut in a white layer, with a brown base layer

> *An Arundel gem (Cat. Thec. A, 140)*

336 AN INTAGLIO; Thetis borne on a Triton conveying the arms to her son. Roman work; deeply cut in a red cornelian

337 HEAD OF DIOMED; a cameo, with the character of a Roman work, cut in a sardonyx out of a white layer on a base of sard

> *One of the Medina gems (Bessb. Cat. No. 40 M)*

338 ACHILLES AND CHIRON. The Centaur is giving the young Achilles a lesson on the lyre; a Cupid behind is listening. Perhaps a work of the 2nd century: it is deeply cut in intaglio on a fine sard

339 AN INTAGLIO OF ACHILLES AND A CENTAUR; rather late Roman work, as seen by the material in which it is engraved, a red jasper

> *One of the Chesterfield gems acquired by Lord Bessborough (Cat. No. 31 c)*

F

340 Two Figures, engraved in intaglio on a very fine and large yellow sard, representing, perhaps, Paris and Œnone. The figures are nude, and are not therefore (as the Blenheim Catalogue interprets them) Phaon and Sappho. The gem is fine work, and cut by an antique hand. In gold enamelled border

Mr. King considers the figures to represent a muse and comic poet

The gem was once Mariette's; see Caylus, Rec. 1, p. 129

340a An Intaglio, that seems to be a modern copy on a reduced scale of the Paris and Œnone, No. 340; stated by a note in the Duke of Marlborough's handwriting to have been engraved by Natter. It is cut on quartz

341 An Intaglio on a Deep-Coloured Sard (or sardine) of the large dimensions of ¾ inch by 1 1/12 inch. It represents Diomed and Ulysses seizing the Palladium. Diomed on one side is seated on a cippus, in the attitude so often repeated upon gems, holding the talismanic image in his left, and his sword in his right hand (as viewed on an impression). On the other, the left half of the stone (the right on an impression from it), Ulysses, the herald's staff in his left hand and the chlamys on his other arm, points to the body of the priestess at his feet. A figure with a trident (of Poseidon?) surmounts a tall column that divides the gem and separates the two heroes; while the wall of the temple-precinct is seen over Ulysses' head.

On the cippus in the signature ΦΗΛΙΞ ΕΠΟΙΕΙ, and in the field over the head of Diomed, as if to balance in the design the wall on the other side, are the words ΚΑΛΠΟΥΡΝΙΟΥ ΘΕΟΥΗΡΟΥ, the name, perhaps of the owner. This important and remarkable gem is one of the very few that the scepticism of Stephani allowed as carrying a genuine signature. Dr. Brunn, while admitting this verdict, has been, with Stephani, misled as to the position of the inscriptions. Worlidge has made no such error. The position of this intaglio in this Collection as an Arundelian gem secures it from the charge of being a forgery of the last century; and there seems no valid ground for withholding from this remarkable intaglio the title Brunn has allowed to it of ancient workmanship. It was probably a work of the age of Hadrian

An Arundel gem (Ar. Cat. Thec. E, No. 2)

Figured in the "Marlborough Gems," vol. i. No. 39, and by Worlidge in his Etchings, No. 52, where he has put the inscriptions in their correct positions

342 INTAGLIO. Diomed, master of the Palladium: a Renaissance work, on an agate

An Arundel gem (Cat. Thec. E, No. 9)

343 A GEM IN INTAGLIO, with the singular lettering ΔΙΟΓΗΝΕΣ. The dress is that of Ulysses—the pilos and chiton. The work is apparently of a good Roman period of art, on a nicolo

Æneas.

344 AN INTAGLIO OF APOLLO HELPING ÆNEAS (who is only represented by his last retreating leg) to escape from Diomed through the Scœan gate: Diomed is striking at a cloud unrepresented in the gem

It is a fine work, cut in a rich and uniform sard, square in form with the angles rounded, and set in a light and beautiful ring of 18th Century workmanship

It was from the Medina Collection (Bessb. Cat. No. 21 M). It seems to have belonged to Caylus in 1762. See his "Thec. d'Antiquités," V., Pl. liii. 3

Figured by Worlidge, No. 17, and in the "Marlborough Gems," vol. i. No. 46

344 bis. DIOMED AND ÆNEAS AT THE SCŒAN GATE: the same subject as the last, but cut in cameo on a good sardonyx

Natter figured and described the last gem, No. 344, in his Treatise

F 2

345 ÆNEAS CARRYING ANCHISES AND CONDUCTING ASCANIUS. An intaglio worked during the good Roman period, on a fine pale sard

346 Two WARRIORS CONVERSING, PYLADES AND ORESTES? An intaglio on a sard. Mr. King terms them Achilles and Antilochus, and considers the work as late Greek

An Arundel gem (Cat. Thec. A, No. 62)

347 AN INTAGLIO: Tydeus with the head of Melanippus. An Etruscan or early Greek work on a sard. On the reverse is a Victory

A Bessborough gem (Cat. No. 52)

348 IPHIGENIA OR POLYXENA OFFERED IN SACRIFICE: a Roman intaglio on a sard

An Arundel gem (Cat. Thec. A, No. 79)

349 A FULL-FACED HEAD OF LAOCOON, cut on a rich amethyst in cameo in the last century. It was, in fact, engraved by Sirletti, according to Marietto

A Bessborough gem (Cat. No. 21)

Figured in the " Marlborough Gems," vol. i. No. 25

350 A VERY FINE SHELL CAMEO OF LAOCOON. The drawing and design are admirable, and the work probably of the 17th century, perhaps even by the hand of Fiamingo.

See Illustration, p. 48

II. ICONOGRAPHY.

351 AN INTAGLIO HEAD OF HOMER, to tho right. A beautiful and delicate Greek work, on a fine yellow sard, representing tho conventional features of the poet

352 A VERY SMALL CAMEO ; a head, to the right, representing Sappho ; very like in profile and head-dress to the Sappho heads on the small electrum coins of Lesbos. It is cut in a white layer on a reddish base, and is probably Greek work. In gold ring with ruby on each side of bezel

One of the Medina gems in the Bessborough Collection (Cat. No. 10 M)

353 INTAGLIO ON A PLASMA. A female head, to tho left, tied with ribbons in a stylo usually attributed to Sappho. Mounted as a seal

One of the gems originally Lord Chesterfield's (Besb. Cat. No. 24 c)

354 AN INTAGLIO HEAD, to tho right, of Socrates, on dark jasper. Fino work, probably of tho early Imperial time

355 A ROMAN INTAGLIO ON A CORNELIAN ; a head, to tho right, that seems meant for Socrates

356 AN INTAGLIO ; Socrates and Plato, on a fine almandine garnet, being a representation of the heads of the two philosophers, confronting one another. A precise duplicate of this fine gem on a poor cornelian is in the Bibliothèque Impériale at Paris. Both gems have all the appearance of being Greco-Roman work of the early Imperial age. This cabochon almandine belonged to the Earl of Chesterfield before falling into the Bessborough Collection

(Bessb. Cat. No. 7 c.) Figured by Worlidge, 83, and in "Marlborough Gems," vol. ii. No. 3

357 An Intaglio, head of Plato, on a fine brown sard, to the left, fine Roman work

358 Cameo Head of Alexander the Great, to the right. The helmet is ornamented in very low relief by a combat between one [warrior and another in a chariot drawn by gryphons. It probably was wrought in its entirety in the time of Caracalla or of Severus Alexander. The stone is a fine sardonyx, of which a clear white layer forms the face, in relief upon a black ground; a surface layer of a red colour forming the helmet.

An Arundel gem (Cat. Thec. C, No. 5)
Figured in the " Marlborough Gems," vol. ii. No. 4
See Illustration

359 A Beautiful Little Cameo, representing Alexander the Great. The face, to the right, is in an opaque white layer on a base of horny chalcedony

360 The Same Subject, to the right, with Pichler's signature ΠΙΧΛΕΡ. This cameo is on a fine sardonyx; the Ammon horn standing out in a surface layer of a rich brown colour

361 A Cameo, carrying what is probably meant to be a bust, to the right, of Alexander the Great

362 A Helmeted Head of Rather Deep Intaglio, three-quarter face, of the type usually called "Hannibal." It might be rather late Italo-Greek work. It is on a good sard, and is a beautiful gem

363 Same Subject, cut in intaglio on a large agate, either a Renaissance work, or of the last century

A Bessborough gem (Cat. No. 35)
Etched by Worlidge, No. 16, and figured in the " Marlborough Gems," vol. ii. No. 20

364 An Admirable Portrait of Demetrius III., Philopator. It is in the style of the contemporary Greek work, being cut in a shallow manner on a sard; the head to the right. In chased ring with a diamond on either shoulder

Figured by Worlidge, in his Etchings, as a Tiberius

No. 423.

No. 401.

No. 358.

No. 416.

No. 185.

365 A SMALL CAMEO, intended for the last of the Ptolemies. The hair is in a yellow and dark brown layer; the face, which is to the right, is in white, on a greyish translucent base. It is set in an open mounting of silver with small diamonds

366 AN EGYPTIAN QUEEN, in the vulture head-dress, as a priestess of Isis; called a Cleopatra. The face and head, to the left, are cut in a rich brown layer of sard on a white base. The work is of a grand and bold order, admirable in polish. This cameo is probably the Ptolemaic-Greek original of many copies. In open frame setting adorned with precious stone

It was from the Bessborough Collection (Cat. No. 2), and called an Isis

Figured in the " Marlborough Gems," vol. ii. No. 17

367 A CAMEO, probably by a French artist, representing a bust of Cleopatra full-faced, and in the conventional modern type; on an onyx. Set in ring with border of diamonds

End of Second Day's Sale.

Third Day's Sale.

On WEDNESDAY, JUNE 28, 1899,

AT ONE O'CLOCK PRECISELY.

(2.) *ROMAN AND POST-AUGUSTAN PORTRAITURE.*

368 AN INTAGLIO ON A SARD, meant perhaps to represent Lucius
Junius Brutus ; a head to the left

> *One of the Chesterfield gems (Cat. No. 21 c, " Metrodorus ")*
> *Figured in the " Marlborough Gems," vol. ii. No. 2, as*
> *Metrodorus, and also by Worlidge, No. 34*

369 THE SAME SUBJECT, to the left, an intaglio, cut in a convex
sard

> *Perhaps an Arundel gem (Ar. Cat. Thec. A, 11)*

370 AN INTAGLIO ON A BRIGHT RED SARD. A helmeted head in
three-quarter face with the lettering M. RE. ATI., and
intended to represent Marcus Atilius Regulus

> *An Arundel gem (Cat. Thec. A, 12)*

371 AN INTAGLIO OF THE SAME AGE AS THE LAST, on a sard,
lettered COS VII and meant for Caius Marius ; the head
to the right

> *An Arundel gem (Cat. Thec. A, No. 10)*

372 AN INTAGLIO ON A FINE LITTLE SAPPHIRE, representing Cicero :
the head to the left

> *From the Chesterfield Collection (Bessb. Cat. No. 11 c)*

373 AN INTAGLIO ON RED JASPER, representing a portrait of Sextus
Pompeius ; the head to the left. In gold ring, chased

  *A Bessborough gem (Cat. No. 53), termed Ptolemy the
  Great*

874 AN INTAGLIO OF GOOD ROMAN WORK, meant probably for Sextus
Pompeius ; the head is to the left, on a sard

  An Arundel gem (Cat. Thec. A, No. 13)

375 A PORTRAIT IN PROFILE, to the left, of Marcus Junius Brutus.
It is a beautifully worked intaglio on a rich little sard. The
form of the head is somewhat different from that represented
on the coins, but it is without doubt intended for his portrait,
and it is certainly Roman work not later than the early
Imperial time. In enamelled gold ring

  From the Chesterfield Collection (Bessb. Cat. No. 3 c)
  *Figured in the " Marlborough Gems," vol. i. No. 4, and by
  Worlidge, No. 10*

376 THE ABOVE, copied on a beautiful sard in modern times ; interesting from the contrast the work affords to its antique
prototype

  From the Bessborough Collection (Cat. No. 55)

377 AN INTAGLIO ON A VERY FINE NICOLO, probably representing
Lucius Junius Brutus ; a head to the left, by a Renaissance
hand. Mounted in gold as a seal

  An Arundel gem (Thec. A, No. 146)

378 MARK ANTONY ; an intaglio on a fine golden sard. The face,
to the right, is somewhat less hard in feature than on coins,
and thus bears some resemblance to Vespasian. It seems a
contemporary work, and in the finest manner, of the Græco-
Roman period

379 AN INTAGLIO, probably of Lepidus, on a bright red sard ; good
work, probably of the early Imperial age ; the head to the
left

380 A HEAD, to the left, of Julius Cæsar on a nicolo

381 An Intaglio. The same subject with still less of the character of Julius Cæsar. A work remarkable for the stone that it is upon—a sapphire; the head is to the left

> An Arundel gem (Cat. Thec. A, No. 15)

382 Intaglio. The same head, to the left, on a magnificent nicolo. Mounted in gold as a seal

> A Bessborough gem (Cat. No. 19)
>
> Figured in the " Marlborough Gems," vol. i. No. 3

383 A Portrait, probably meant for Julius Cæsar. A nice intaglio, the head to the right, on a sapphire

> One of the Bessborough gems (Cat. No. 48)

384 An Intaglio Head, probably meant for Julius Cæsar, engraved in a large sard by some cinque-cento hand; the head to the left

> An Arundel gem (Cat. Thec. E, No. 12)

385 A Small Statuette Bust, cut out of a magnificent hyacinthine sard, as beautiful for colour as for transparency. It is called Nerva, but is probably meant for Julius Cæsar, and would seem to be a work of the fine period of the cinque-cento

> It was an Arundel gem (Cat. Thec. E, No. 16)
>
> Figured in the " Marlborough Gems," vol. i. No. 17

386 Intaglio of Augustus very Young; a head to the left. Good Roman work, on a hyacinthine sard

> A Bessborough gem (Cat. No. 2 c)
>
> Figured by Worlidge and in the " Marlborough Gems," vol. i. No. 6, and called there a Lepidus

387 A Fragment, being part of a portrait of Augustus, to the left, in the character of Hermes, a caduceus being in the field; in shallow intaglio. When complete it must have been some 3 inches high by nearly 2 inches broad. It is cut in a brown sard, and delicately finished

> This gem seems to have been one of those acquired by the third Duke, and is figured in the " Marlborough Gems," vol. ii. No. 16

No. 390.

No. 390.

388 AN INTAGLIO OF CONSIDERABLE MERIT, on a sard, representing Augustus in apotheosis; the head to the left, no doubt studied from the large brass coins. Mounted as a seal

389 A FINE CAMEO, in a splendid nicolo, of a head of Augustus. A rim is reserved, formed in the upper bluish layer of the stone

390 A CAMEO, nearly three inches in height. Head, looking to the right, of the deified Augustus (with the radiate crown); extremely fine work. The emperor's head is left in a porcelain-white layer in relief, on a reddish-brown sard under layer; altogether a noble gem of the period of the early empire. The setting of this cameo is a beautifully chased and elaborate framework, with cartouche ornaments, &c. in various coloured enamel; the back, also beautifully enamelled, has a border of scale-pattern, &c.; wrought probably in the cinque-cento period

Figured in the "Marlborough Gems," vol. i. No. 7

See Illustration

391 A CAMEO, representing probably Augustus deified. The head is seen in front face, veiled, and in the highest relief. It i cut in an opaque white porcelain-like layer, but the ground has been fractured, cut off, and substituted by gold. It is a noble Roman work, 1¾ inches high by 1 inch in width. In open frame setting mounted with precious stones

From the Bessborough Collection (Cat. No. 3)

Figured in the "Marlborough Gems," vol. i. No. 8

392 A CAMEO, in very high relief apparently representing Augustus when young, crowned with a laurel wreath. It is very beautiful work. The features are carved in a fine porcelain-white stratum of an onyx, 1½ inch high by 1 inch wide; the base is brown. In open frame setting mounted with precious stones

From the Bessborough Collection (Cat. No. 4)

Figured in the "Marlborough Gems," vol. i. No. 12, as Germanicus

393 A SMALL CAMEO, on sardonyx, representing the head of young Augustus, looking to the left, in a white layer on a brown ground

394 AN ANTIQUE CAMEO, representing the same subject as the last,
looking to the right; cut in an opaque yellow layer of an
onyx with a bluish-grey base

395 A CAMEO, representing Augustus laureated in a clear amethystine chalcedony with an opaline foil, and mounted in an
enamelled slide, *temp.* Louis XIII.

An Arundel gem (Cat. Thec. B, No. 21)

396 A FINE CAMEO, probably representing the head of Augustus to
the left, in a pale coffee-tinted layer, on a dark bluish-grey
base

396A A VERY FINE CAMEO, in high relief, nearly front-faced bust,
probably also of Augustus, in an opaque white layer on a
pinkish-grey ground

397 A PASTE CAMEO, white on black ground, perhaps also meant for
Augustus; the head to the left

398 A CAMEO, of beautiful workmanship, representing a profile head
of Augustus to the left, cut on a whitish layer on a bluish
base. In gold ring, the bezel set with diamonds

399 A PROFILE AND BUST, to the right, representing Livia. It is a
small cameo of Roman workmanship, on a sardonyx

400 A MINUTE CAMEO; a small female veiled head to the right,
cut on a sardonyx, the face in a white layer, the veil in a
yellow surface layer, on a base of jet black. It is good,
probably Roman work, and may represent Livia; mounted in
a tasteful blue enamelled ring, adorned with stars

An Arundel gem (Cat. Thec. A, No. 109)

401 A BUST, of Livia, veiled, and in front face, represented as Ceres.
A cameo on a sardonyx, in very high relief, carved in a
porcelain-white layer, on a mottled sard base. The gem is
1¾ inch in height.

An Arundel gem (Cat. Thec. C, No. 7)
Figured in the " Marlborough Gems," vol. ii. 24
See Illustration, p. 66

402 A FEMALE HEAD AND PART OF BUST, to the left; possibly
Livia, in the character of Ceres. A cameo on a sardonyx,
the hair and veil in a jet black layer; the face in a white
stratum, with the base layer black. It may be a Ceres,
however, of the age of Severus; the work being of the rude
type then prevalent. It is prettily set, like 446, in a gold
wire looped border

Perhaps the Arundel gem (Cat. Thec. A, No. 124)

403 A CAMEO, of extraordinary beauty and interest; Livia and the
young Tiberius, in green turquoise. The work as perfect
as the stone is remarkable. It is without doubt a gem of
the Augustan age

It was in the Bessborough Collection (Cat. p. 27)
*It is exquisitely figured in the " Marlborough Gems," vol. i.
No. 10*

404 AN INTAGLIO HEAD, to the left, on cornelian; very good work,
probably meant for the young Tiberius

405 A CAMEO HEAD, cut in a white layer on a yellow sard ground,
apparently meant for Tiberius. The portrait looks to the
left

*An Arundel gem (Cat. Thec. A, No. 108), termed Drusus,
son of Tiberius*
Figured in the " Marlborough Gems," vol. ii. No. 25

406 A CAMEO, 1¼ inch in height, by nearly 1 inch in width. A
bust of the young Tiberius to the left; the face rendered in
white layer, the wreath and shoulder in a yellow-brown
layer, on a mould of mottled yellow chalcedony. Fine
Roman work. In gold mount

From the Bessborough Collection (Cat. No. 6)

407 A CAMEO, 3 inches in height by 1¾ in width, probably meant
to represent Tiberius, the portrait being much like his coins
struck in Asia Minor. The face, a portrait to the right, is
cut in a bluish-white layer on a translucent base of yellowish
chalcedony. Mounted in a moulded gold rim, with loop.

See Illustration, p. 86

408 A MINUTE CAMEO ; a head to the left, in a yellowish layer of a sardonyx, with a grey base. It probably represents Marcus Agrippa, and would seem to be contemporary work

409 THE SAME SUBJECT, with the rostral crown ; the portrait is to the left, in a white layer of an onyx on a translucent base
Figured in the " Marlborough Gems," vol. ii. No. 23

410 A LARGE BLOODSTONE CAMEO, 3 inches high by 2½ inches in width. A head to the left intended for Agrippa

411 A " MARCELLUS," on a wonderfully fine hyacinthine garnet, from the cameo No. 412. The head is to the right

412 A CAMEO ; a head in a white layer on a grey ground, looking to the left ; perhaps meant for Marcellus
An Arundel gem (Cat. Thec. A, No. 116)
Figured in the " Marlborough Gems," vol. i. No. 9, *as Marcellus*

413 A CAMEO PORTRAIT, in shallow relief to the left, in a white layer on a black base. A Renaissance work intended for Drusus
Apparently the Arundel gem (Cat. Thec. A, No. 120)
Figured in the " Marlborough Gems," vol. i. No. 11

414 A CAMEO, on a sardonyx, 1¾ inch high by 1½ inch wide. A fine laureated head to the right ; the laurel wreath and robe in a rich yellow layer ; flesh in a pure white layer, on a ground of yellowish brown. Possibly intended for Antonia, but the likeness is not very strong. It is, however, good Roman work of the Imperial age. In gold frame
An Arundel gem (Cat. Thec. C, No. 2)
Figured in the " Marlborough Gems," vol. ii. No. 27

415 CONJOINED HEADS OF GERMANICUS AND AGRIPPINA, to the left. Cinque-cento work on an onyx, cut in a white layer on a bluish-grey base
An Arundel gem (Cat. Thec. B, No. 3)

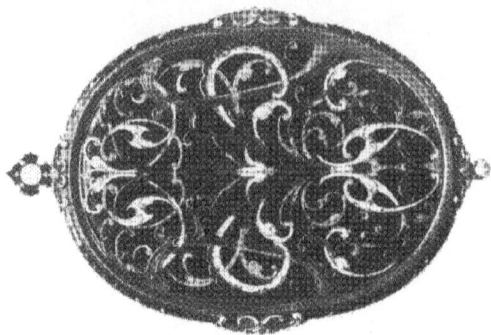

No. 422

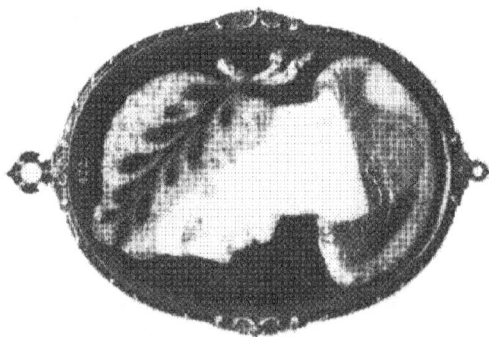

No. 422.

416 CAMEO ON A SARDONYX, 1⅞ inch in height by 1¼ inch in width.
A head of Agrippina the older to the right. The richly
worked hair and laurel wreath is cut in a fine brown layer;
the face in a bluish-white stratum on a dark base. The
work is very fine, and worthy of the magnificent stone on
which it is cut. It is a noble gem of the Augustan age.
Set in a gold mount, with moulded edge, chased and
enamelled in black; the back has an elaborate arabesque
design on black enamelled ground

   An Arundel gem (Cat. Thec. D, No. 2)
   See Illustration, p. 66

417 AN INTAGLIO PORTRAIT OF AGRIPPINA THE YOUNGER, to the left,
lightly veiled as Ceres, below bust, ACΠACIOY, on a splendid
red sard, an inch in height

   One of the Medina gems (Bessb. Cat. No. 14 м)
   Figured by Worlidge, and in the "Marlborough Gems,"
   vol. i. No. 14

418 A COPY, signed by Pichler, from the sitting statue of Agrippina
in the Villa Albani. A pretty cameo

419 CAMEO, entirely in sard; a head of Caius Cæsar. Excellent and
antique work, set in a brass ring

   An Arundel gem (Cat. Thec. A, No. 110)

420 AN INTAGLIO PORTRAIT, to the left, on a pale sapphire; probably
meant for the young Caligula. It is set in a fine massive
mediæval ring

   An Arundel gem (Cat. Thec. C, No. 17)

421 A CAMEO, representing Caligula; a head, to the left, in a black
layer on a greyish-brown ground

   An Arundel gem (Ar. Cat. Thec. B, No. 19)

422 A CAMEO, representing Claudius Cæsar, to the left, with an
oaken crown and the paludamentum. It is cut on a sardonyx 2⅞ inches high by 2 inches wide. The flesh is rendered in a porcelain-white layer, the wreath and ægis in a
reserved stratum of fine yellow, while the base is also composed of yellow sard. The work is probably contemporary.
Set in a gold mount, the border of leaf-pattern, with chased
cartouche ornaments at sides, enamelled in white, green
and black; the back of the mount is pierced à jour with an
elaborate arabesque design richly enamelled in colours

   An Arundel gem termed Britannicus (Ar. Cat. Thec.D,No. 9)
   See Illustration

423 A CAMEO BUST OF CLAUDIUS, to the right, on a fine sardonyx, 2⅛ inches high by 1¾ inch wide; the face being cut in a translucent bluish-white layer, the hair in a whiter stratum, the civic oak wreath and the paludamentum in a rich brown sard layer, and the base consisting of tortoiseshell sard. The work is much the same quality as that in No. 422, and seems to be contemporary with the emperor. It is set in a rim of plain gold

    An Arundel gem (Cat. Thec. C, No. 11)

    See Illustration, p. 66,

424 A SMALL FRONT-FACE PORTRAIT OF MESSALINA, in cameo, in high relief, on a lapis lazuli

425 AN INTAGLIO PORTRAIT OF NERO, to the left, at about twenty-four years of age, on a fragment of sard. The likeness is good and the work contemporary

    An Arundel gem (Cat. Thec. A, No. 18)

426 A SMALL CAMEO HEAD OF NERO, to the left. Contemporary work. The head in a white layer on a greyish-black ground. Mounted in gold ring, the bezel set with diamonds

    An Arundel gem (Cat. Thec. A, No. 107)

427 CAMEO, 1¾ inch high by 1 inch wide, carrying a head of Nero, to the left; cut in a wax-like pinkish layer in middle relief, on a somewhat yellow opaque base. It is fine work, and probably contemporary

428 A SMALL RENAISSANCE CAMEO, representing a head of Nero, to the right; in a white layer on a grey ground

429 A SMALL ONYX CAMEO, head of Nero, to the right; in a white layer on a grey ground

430 A SMALL CAMEO, on sardonyx, with the same subject, to the left; in a yellow-brown layer on a white base

    An Arundel gem (Cat. Thec. B, No. 27)

431 SMALL CAMEO, on an amethyst? perhaps Nero, but possibly Domitian, and described as such in the Arundel Catalogue

    An Arundel gem (Cat. Thec. A, No. 115) ?— described as on a garnet

No. 436.

432 ONYX : small cameo, head of Nero, to the left, in a white layer
on a grey ground

433 SARDONYX ; a very fine cameo, representing the laureated head of
Galba, to the left, being a fragment of a larger gem. It is
1½ inch high by 1 inch wide, in a marble white layer, on a
black base

An Arundel gem (Cat. Thec. A, No. 123)

Figured in the " Marlborough Gems, vol. i. No. 16

434 ONYX ; a small cameo head of Galba, to the right. Probably
contemporary ; in a white layer on a bluish-grey base

An Arundel gem (Cat. Thec. A, No. 117)

435 ONYX ; a small cameo, ⅗ths of an inch high, representing perhaps
Galba, or it may be Vespasian, to the right. A finely
worked little gem ; the face cut in a dead white layer on a
black base

436 AN EXTRAORDINARY SARDONYX, 3½ inches high by 2⅞ inches
wide, engraved with a helmeted head and bust, in rather low
relief. Portrait of Andrea Carafa, Count of Sanseverino,
Viceroy of Naples, 1525–1526. (See medal engraved in the
Tresor Numismatique, vol. ii. XXXIII.) The base of the
stone consists of deep red, almost black sard ; the face and
crest of the helmet and neck are worked in a white layer,
while the helmet and coat of mail are reserved in an upper
layer of deep brown hue. Round the head has been written
in characters not engraved but stained into the stone, the
words : ANDREAS CARRAFA SANCTA SEVERINA COMES. This
lettering can be seen by strong sun-light, or by breathing
on the stone, and illustrates the singular porosity that
characterises chalcedony, even in the form of the finest sard.
In an elaborate openwork frame of gold set with peridot,
jacinth, sapphires, &c.

This splendid sardonyx was in the Bessborough Collection
(Cat. No. 15)

See Illustration

G

437 AN ONYX CAMEO, representing Galba to the right; a very nice
work of the cinque-cento period; cut on a stone 1½ inch in
height in a white stratum on a horn-like base

An Arundel gem (Cat. Thec. B, No. 40)
Figured in the "Marlborough Gems," vol. i. No. 16

438 ONYX CAMEO. A small head, probably meant for Galba, to the
left

439 ONYX CAMEO. Head of Otho, in a white layer on a dark grey
ground

An Arundel gem (Cat. Thec. A, No. 118)

440 YELLOWISH CHALCEDONY. A small intaglio head of Vespasian,
to the left. It is mounted in a very pretty enamelled ring

An Arundel gem (Cat. Thec. A, No. 19)

441 RED JASPER. Head of Vespasian to the left

442 SMALL CAMEO ON ONYX. A head of Vespasian, to the right, in
a white layer on a dark base

An Arundel gem (Cat. Thec. A, No. 121)

443 SARDONYX. A small cinque-cento cameo, mounted in a very
pretty ring, representing Vespasian, to the right, in a white
layer on a bluish-grey ground, with laurel wreath in a yellow
layer, and a rim in the white layer

An Arundel gem (Cat. Thec. A, No. 106)

444 ONYX. A stone 1⅘ inch high by 1¼ inch wide. A three-
quarter face head of Vespasian; against a flesh coloured
under layer the face is seen in white with a slight tint of
flesh colour. In metal-gilt frame, set with stones

445 AN INTAGLIO ON A LARGE PLASMA, 1¼ inch high by ⅞ inch
wide. Head of Titus to the right

An Arundel gem (Cat. Thec. E, No. 20)

446 SARDONYX. A cameo, representing probably the head of Titus, to the left, taken from his Alexandrian coins, in a bluish-white translucent layer, and reserved rim on a yellowish-brown base. The work is enclosed in a beautiful gold wire setting, similar to that of No. 402, and in style resembling those of Nos. 452 and 461

An Arundel gem (Cat. Thec. A, No. 125), *called Vespasian*

447 AN INTAGLIO ON A SPLENDID HYACINTHINE SARD. The renowned bust of the daughter of Titus by Nicander, whereof the upper part of the head and the head-dress are restored in gold. Mr. King considers it to be a Berenice, but the comparison with coins seems to justify the original attribution. The inscription is beyond all suspicion genuine, and might be of Ptolemaic date. It is retrograde

NIKANΔP.<
ⲤⲚ.ⲤⲒ

The portrait is to the left, and the signature behind the neck. The original height of the gem must have been 1½ inch, its width ⅞ nearly. The work is bold and doubtless contemporary with the personage it represents

It was formerly in the Deringh Collection

448 INTAGLIO ON A SARD. A head, to the left, of Domitian when very young. Probably a contemporary work

A Bessborough gem (Cat. No. 107)

449 A CAMEO ON AN ONYX, representing Domitian, to the right, with the fine workmanship of the cinque-cento period. The relief is cut in a white porcelain-like layer on a pale base

450 A BEAUTIFUL PLASMA. An intaglio to the left, representing Domitia Longina, the wife of Domitian

Bought by the third Duke from the jeweller Lavocat

451 ONYX; a minute cameo, representing Domitian, to the right; in a white layer on a dark-grey ground

An Arundel gem (Ar. Cat. Thec. B, No. 24)

G 2

452 SARDONYX; 1⅝ inch high by 1¾ inch wide. A cameo bust to the left, of probably Trajan, senior; dressed with the cuirass, carrying the Gorgoneion, perhaps in the garb of a general. In rather flat relief, cut in a white layer over a light brown stratum of the stone. It is set in a gold wire setting with a row of garnets

Figured in the " Marlborough Gems," vol. ii. No. 21, *as Sulla*

An Arundel gem (Ar. Cat. Thec. C, No. 13), *termed Gordian jun.*

453 A PASTE COPY OF No. 454

454 INTAGLIO HEAD, to the left, of Sabina, or possibly Marciana, on a rich sard. A fine work, probably contemporary

From the Chesterfield Collection (Bessb. Cat. No. 1 c), *called by Natter, Plotina or Marciana*

Figured in the " Marlborough Gems," vol. i. No. 19, *as Marciana*

455 ON A FINE RED SARD. An intaglio head of Sabina, to the right. Very fine contemporary work

Figured in the " Marlborough Gems," vol. i. No. 20, *and etched by Worlidge*

456 ON A FINE YELLOW SARD. A head of Sabina in intaglio

457 ON A MOTTLED YELLOWISH CHALCEDONY. A full-faced representation, carved in the round, of Marciana, the sister of Trajan, in apotheosis. This important gem, the dimensions of which are 3 inches in height and width, represents the empress in bust, as if seated on a peacock. This gem, which must have been a work of Trajan's age, was once in the collection of the Dukes of Mantua

A Medina gem, called by Natter, in the Catalogue of the Bessborough Gems (Cat. No. 37 M), *Domitia. It is figured under this name, too, in the " Marlborough Gems," vol. ii. No.* 28. *Domitia, however, died after her husband, and in private life, and could hardly have been thus canonised. Marciana, on the other hand, received the honours of the apotheosis, as coins of the " consecratio " exist*

See Illustration, p. 17

458 INTAGLIO ON A GARNET. Head of Hadrian, to the left. Apparently a good contemporary work.

459 ON A SARDONYX. A small bust of Mercury, to the left, with imitation of an Etruscan border round it. The intaglio, which appears to be Roman work, is cut in a brown layer, below which there is a white layer resting on a black base, the stone being bevelled down to exhibit the strata

460 ON A SARDONYX. A small bust of Hadrian, to the left. Cameo. The topmost layer is of a fine coral red, to which a white stratum succeeds with a grey base

461 A CAMEO IN AN ONYX. A head of Hadrian, to the right. A very good work cut in a pinkish-white layer on a mottled, reddish base. It is 1½ inch high by 1¾ inch wide. Set as No. 452

Figured in the "Marlborough Gems," vol. ii. No. 29

An Arundel gem, called a Balbinus in the Catalogue (Thec. C, No. 14)

462 INTAGLIO ON A PALE YELLOW SARD. Very fine head of Antoninus Pius, to the left. This rare portrait is in the best Roman work of his time. In enamelled ring

One of the Chesterfield gems (Cat. No. 45 c)

463 ON A YELLOWISH SARD. Intaglio head, probably meant for Antoninus Pius, to the left. Of late Roman work

An Arundel gem (Cat. Thec. A, No. 20)

464 INTAGLIO ON A YELLOWISH SARD. A head to the left, of Faustina Mater, with her usual head-dress, the hair being wreathed up with pearls. It is a portrait in Roman workmanship

465 A SAPPHIRE RING, lined with gold with enamelled edge, engraved with the intaglio portrait of Faustina the elder, to the left. The ring is evidently of Oriental, probably Persian, workmanship, the head of the empress having taken the place of an inscription

An Arundel gem (Cat. Thec. E, No. 15)

466 A CAMEO ON AN AMETHYST, in extremely high relief, representing a full-faced bust of the Empress Faustina the elder.
She is veiled, perhaps as Proserpine. The work is very fine
and contemporary

An Arundel gem (Cat. Thec. C, No. 15)

467 ON A BLUISH TRANSLUCENT CHALCEDONY. A front-faced cameo
bust, in nearly full relief, of Faustina the elder. She is
represented as Juno, her diadem being adorned with real
pearls. It is a work of great beauty. Nearly 1¼ inch in
height. In gold mount with loop

An Arundel gem (Thec. C, No. 17)

468 ON A SINGULAR SARDONYX. A cameo portrait in low relief
representing Faustina the elder, to the right. The upper
layer is pink ; the flesh rendered in a pinkish white, the base
being translucent and pink

From the Arundel Collection (Cat. Thec. B, No. 15)

469 ON A SARDONYX. A cameo head of Faustina the elder, to the
left. Very beautiful work. A bequest to the Duke of
Marlborough from the Duchess of Bedford

470 ON A NICOLO. Portrait to the left of Marcus Aurelius

471 ONYX. · Cameo, with conjoined busts of Marcus Aurelius and
Faustina. Cinque-cento work, in a white layer on a grey
base

An Arundel gem (Cat. Thec. B, No. 8)

472 INTAGLIO ON A SARD. Portrait of Faustina the younger, to the
left

From Lord Chesterfield's Collection (Bessb. Cat. No. 20 c)
Called by Natter, Julia Pia Felix

473 A CAMEO ON A SARDONYX. A small head of Faustina the
younger, to the left. Apparently of Roman workmanship
It is cut in a white layer on a dark sard ground

474 A Sardonyx. A cameo portrait, apparently of Faustina the younger, to the right ; ivy-crowned, in a Bacchanal character. The ivy wreath and the rim are reserved in a brown layer. The work is good. It is 1¾ inch in height by 1 inch

An Arundel gem (Cat. Thec. B, No. 10)

Figured in the "Marlborough Gems," vol. ii. No. 14, *as Libera*

475 On a Sardonyx. A cameo bust attributed to Faustina the younger, to the right. In low relief, exhibiting nevertheless three distinct layers of the stone. Good work

A Bessborough gem (Cat. No. 8)

Figured in the "Marlborough Gems," vol. ii. No. 32, *as Lucilla*

476 On an Onyx. A bust portrait of Faustina the younger, to the right

Figured in the "Marlborough Gems," vol. ii. No. 32, *as Lucilla*

477 Nicolo. A cameo portrait, in low relief, of Lucius Verus, to the left. It is good contemporary work, cut in a bluish-white layer on a black sard base. Set in gold as a pendant, with enamelled border

An Arundel gem (Cat. Thec. C, No. 12), *termed Ælius Cæsar*

478 Onyx, opaque white on grey. Portrait, to the right, in cameo, meant probably for Lucius Verus, of Renaissance work. It is beautifully mounted in a contemporary enamelled setting, with small table diamonds in front, and the back is finely enamelled with a leaf design

A Bessborough gem (Cat. No. 7)

See Illustration, p. 39

479 Fine Brown Sard. A three-quarter bust intaglio, representing Lucilla in the character of Diana. A remarkable gem of good contemporary Roman workmanship

One of the Arundel gems (Cat. Thec. A, No. 90)

480 A MAGNIFICENT SARDONYX, 2½ inches high. It is a nicolo-sardonyx; a summit layer of brown is left only on the cornice, the hair and paludamentum; the work is in a bluish-white on a black sard base; the whole bevelled to show the strata. It represents a fine head of Commodus, to the right, in a cameo. On the reverse is a figure of the IAΩ Abraxas, worked in intaglio, with the inscription ΑΡΔΟΥ ΓΕΝΝΑΙ ΩΔΕΜΕΝΙ ΒΑCΙΛΙCΚΩC.

An Arundel gem, termed a Didius Julian (Cat. Thec. D, No. 11)

481 CAMEO ON A SARDONYX. A three-quarter figure of the young Commodus, to the left. An early gem. It is 1½ inch high by 1¼ inch wide, and is cut in a white layer on a dark sard base

From the Arundel Collection (Cat. Thec. C, No. 10)

482 A CAMEO ON A UNIQUE SEMI-OVAL SARDONYX; of the dimensions of 8¾ inches in width by 6 inches in height, and therefore ranking among the five most important for their magnitude in existence. It is of all these the most remarkable as a stone, if we consider the quality of its four brilliantly-hued layers, and the parallelism in which they lie superposed. The subject, a pair of imperial heads confronted, is designated as Didius Julian and Manlia Scantilla; these names being engraved on escutcheons on the silver-gilt frame which surrounds the stone, and gives it a rectangular form, while also holding together the four fragments into which this extraordinary sardonyx has at some time been broken. A ram's horn adorns the brow of the emperor, while an oaken (ilex) wreath with acorns surrounds the head. The emblems borne by the empress are not less mixed, for twined with an ilex wreath similar to that of the emperor are wheat-ears, pomegranates, and poppy-heads. A slightly Isiac character is imparted to the empress's attire by a large bow-like knot that ties her fringed robe, similar to the knot ornament (nodus Isiacus) of the priestesses of Isis. A small sphendone-formed tiara furthermore surmounts her forehead.

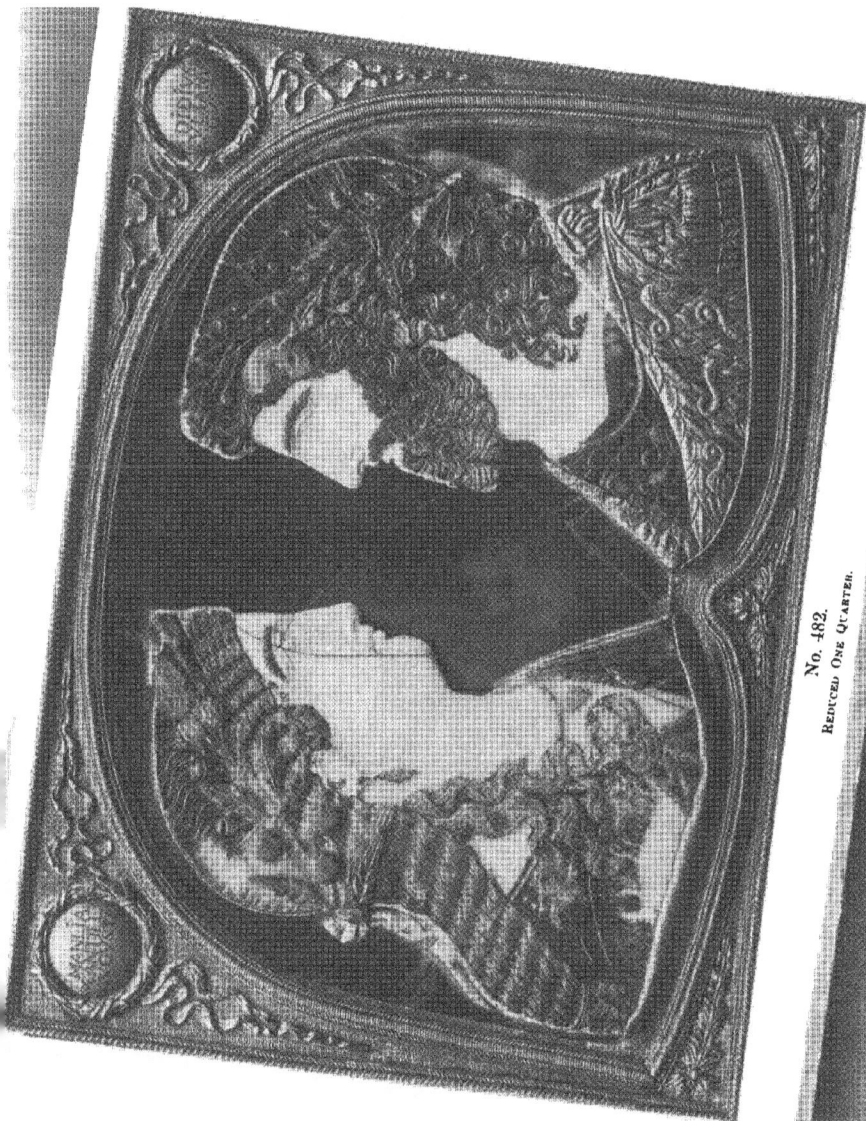

No. 482.
REDUCED ONE QUARTER.

The gem itself we may fairly assume to have been contemporary with the sovereigns it represents.

On the setting at the back of the gem an inscription is seen running as follows : " Ingens anaglyphicum opus olim Saunesiorum ducum nunc vero pretio acquisitum in Fontesiano cimelio asservatum." A Marquis de Fuentes was au ambassador from Portugal in Rome in the earlier half of the last century, and is mentioned by Raspe and by Marietto as a gem collector. From his collection this great gem may have passed to that of the Duke of Marlborough. But to determine to what ducal family it had previously belonged is more difficult.

The work of the cameo is kept in very flat relief, and the artist has otherwise most ingeniously handled his material, so as to give the most contrasted effects to the various layers of the stone

Figured in the " Marlborough Gems "
See Illustration

483 ONYX. A cameo head of Pescennius Niger, to the left
One of the Bessborough gems (Cat. No. 31), *called Antoninus*

484 ON A BERYL. An intaglio bust of Julia Domna, to the left, in the stiff style of her coins. No doubt a work of the first years of the third century. Set as a seal ornamented with diamonds
One of the Bessborough gems (Cat. No. 20)
Figured in the " Marlborough Gems," vol. i. No. 24, *and also among Worlidge's Etchings*

485 ON A REMARKABLE SAPPHIRE, $\frac{3}{8}$ inch high, $\frac{1}{2}$ inch wide. An intaglio portrait of Caracalla, to the left ; indubitably contemporary, and of good workmanship
A gem from the Chesterfield portion of the Bessborough Collection (Cat. No. 8 c). *Worlidge has given an etching of it*

486 ON A VERY FINE SARD. An intaglio portrait, to the right, apparently of the young Caracalla. The form of the paludamentum indicates it as a work of the late Antonine period
An Arundel gem (Cat. Thec. A, No. 37)

487 On a Sard. A portrait in intaglio of the young Caracalla, to the left

> An Arundel gem (Cat. Thec. A, No. 29), called Elagabalus

488 On a Sard, prettily set. An intaglio head, to the left, probably of the young Caracalla

489 On White Oriental Alabaster. A three-quarter face bust, to the right, in very high relief, of Caracalla. The head only is antique, and measures 1½ inch in length

> From the Bessborough Collection (Cat. No. 25)
>
> Figured in the "Marlborough Gems," vol. i. No. 22

490 Onyx. A portrait in cameo of Caracalla, by Pichler, signed ΠΙΧΑΡ ΕΠΟΙΕΙ

491 Fine Pale Plasma; intaglio, three-quarter face. Possibly representing Geta when young, in the character of Mercury. The caduceus is on his left shoulder

492 An Onyx Cameo Portrait, cut in a white layer on a pink-grey ground, to the right, of probably Geta when young

493 On a Pale Citrine. An intaglio profile, to the right, of possibly Elagabalus. He wears a radiate crown and the paludamentum. On the back of the gem a portrait head of a lady is enamelled on a blue enamel ground

> It was one of the Chesterfield gems (Cat. No. 15 c), termed a Ptolemy
>
> Figured in the Marlborough Gems," vol. ii. No. 1, as Ptolemy Auletes. Also among Worlidge's Etchings

494 On an Onyx, in a whitish-blue layer on a dark bluish-grey ground A bust, in high relief, of Elagabalus

> An Arundel gem (Cat. Thec. N, No. 26)

495 A Sardonyx, 3½ inches high by 2½ inches wide. A fine cameo portrait, to the right, of Julia Paula. This important gem appears to be contemporary work of a very high class. The face is worked in a white semi-opaque portion of the upper layer, the rest in a transparent layer, while the ground is a mottled sard

> An Arundel gem, designated as Julia Domna (Cat. Thec. D, No. 8)
>
> See Illustration

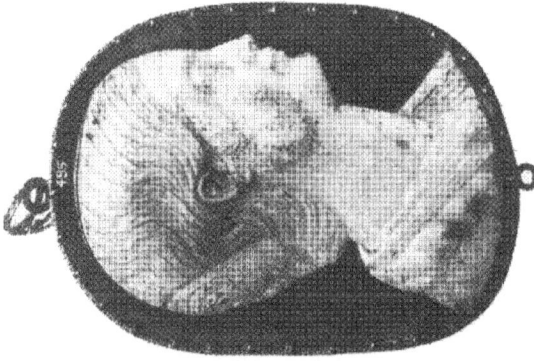

No. 495.

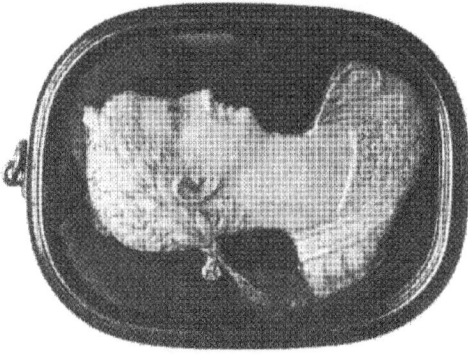

No. 407.

496 A SARDONYX OF THREE LAYERS, 2¼ inches high by 1½ inch wide.
A cameo profile portrait, to the left, of probably Julia
Mamæa, aunt of Elagabalus. The hair and the dress are
carefully and strongly rendered in a massive dark brown
layer. The face, less carefully finished, is in a white layer,
the base layer of the stone being black. It has all the
character of a contemporary work

*Probably the Arundel gem designated **Antonia** (Cat.
Thee. D, No. 3)?*

497 A CAMEO PORTRAIT, to the left. Probably meant for Valerian
An Arundel gem (Cat. Thee. B, No. 32)?

498 FORTY PORTRAIT HEADS, representing the Triumvirs and the
Emperors down to Valerian. Probably by Natter.
The order of the Imperial personages is indicated by
small figures cut on the mountings, corresponding to the
following attributions:

1. Triumvirate.	21. Lucius Verus.
2. Julius Cæsar.	22. Commodus.
3. Marcus Jun. Brutus.	23. Pertinax.
4. Augustus.	24. Didius Julianus.
5. Tiberius.	25. Pescennius Niger.
6. Caligula.	26. Clodius Albinus.
7. Claudius.	27. Septimius Severus.
8. Nero.	28. Caracalla.
9. Galba.	29. Macrinus.
10. Otho.	30. Elagabalus.
11. Vitellius.	31. Alexander Severus.
12. Vespasian.	32. Maximinus.
13. Titus.	33. Gordian Africanus.
14. Domitian.	34. Balbinus and Pupienus.
15. Nerva.	35. Gordian Pius.
16. Trajan.	36. Philip.
17. Hadrian.	37. Trajan Decius.
18. Ælius.	38. Hostilianus.
19. Antoninus Pius.	39. Æmilianus.
20. Marcus Aurelius.	40. Valerianus.

498A A GOLD STATER OF PHILIP II. Mounted as a ring

498B A GOLD STATER OF ALEXANDER. Also mounted as a ring

498c An Oval Cameo, in silver, representing busts of Augustus and Livia; on the reverse the same subject incused. It is a casting of probably cinque-cento date, mounted in an iron ring, with chased gold shoulders and bezel. This identical ring was figured by Gronovius in Gorlæus' " Dactylotheca " in 1609, No. 183

> An Arundel gem (Cat. Thec. A, No. 102)

499 Sardonyx, 1½ inch high by ⅗ths wide. Fine profile portrait to the left, much resembling that attributed to Mæcenas. The head is in an ivory-like upper layer on a yellowish base. The work is very fine, and may be of the Augustan age, and is in considerable relief. It is in a very handsome Renaissance mount, enamelled and set with garnets

> Figured in the " Marlborough Gems," vol. ii. No. 22
>
> See Illustration, p. 101

500 A Large Black Sard, 1½ inch high by 1¼ inch wide. An intaglio, representing a head, to the left, and bust of Antinous with a spear on his left shoulder. The work is magnificent and worthy the age of Hadrian. The letters ANTI remain of what was once a legend. In old mount

> Figured in the " Marlborough Gems," vol. i. No. 21, and in Worlidge's Etchings

500a A Facsimile of the Last, by Burch. Cornelian

501 A Splendid Sard, with an intaglio head to the left; somewhat like Antinous, with his name so inscribed as to read directly, and with the appearance of antiquity. On the back of the gem are the letters LAI, possibly indicating its owner at a period subsequent to the date of its production

> Figured in the " Marlborough Gems," vol. ii. No. 30

501a A Cameo Bust of Antinous, to the right, probably of the cinque-cento period

> An Arundel gem (Cat. Thec. B, No. 4)

502 Chalcedony. A head of Antinous to the right. Fine work of the last century

503 A Fine Yellow Sard. Portrait, to the left, of the Antinous of the bas-relief of the Villa Albani. It is very fine intaglio, and carries the signature of Marchant

(3.) *PORTRAITURE OF UNKNOWN OR UNCERTAIN ATTRIBUTION.*

504 A CORNELIAN: an intaglio. Head to the left, representing the so-called Genius of the Museum Clementinum. It is a deeply-cut work by Marchant, but not signed by him

505 INTAGLIO, to the right; on a sardonyx. A male head of an unknown personage, excellently finished in a Greek or Greco-Roman style. Natter took it for a Brutus; it has a slight beard

    A Bessborough gem (Cat. No. 46)

506 INTAGLIO ON A YELLOWISH SARD. Front face male beardless portrait. A work probably contemporary with the person it represents; the treatment of the hair seems to belong to the end of the first century

    Figured in the "Marlborough Gems," vol. ii. No. 9
    A Bessborough gem (Cat. No. 79)

507 INTAGLIO ON A SARD. Male head, to the left, portrait of an unknown personage, apparently of the Augustan period

    A Bessborough gem, termed by Natter (Cat. No. 81) Cicero
    Figured under the same name in the "Marlborough Gems," vol. ii No. 12, and also among Worlidge's Etchings

508 INTAGLIO ON A BLUISH CHALCEDONY. Portrait, to the right, of Oliver Cromwell

    A Bessborough gem, described by Natter (Cat. No. 90) as a head of " Oliver Cromwell, à l'antique "

509 INTAGLIO ON A PALE PLUM-BLUE AMETHYST. A portrait, to the right, of an unknown head; mounted in an enamelled setting. The work seems of Imperial Roman time

    It is termed Nerva by Natter (Cat. No. 4 c) in his description of the Bessborough Collection, into which it came from the cabinet of Lord Chesterfield
    Figured in the "Marlborough Gems," vol. i. No. 18

510 INTAGLIO ON A RED JASPER. A head, to the left, apparently
representing a barbarian, slightly bearded. It seems to be
work of a good Imperial age. In chased setting, with diamonds at shoulders

> A *Chesterfield gem* (*Cat. No. 12 c*), *termed by Natter a
> Tiberius*

511 INTAGLIO ON A SARD : a portrait, looking to the left, of an
unknown bearded person. The work is vigorous and
probably of the Imperial age. Mounted as a seal

> A *Chesterfield gem* (*Cat. No. 25 c*)

512 INTAGLIO ON A RED PASTE. A bust portrait, to the left. It
may, perhaps, be Geta Cæsar

513 INTAGLIO ON A FINE SARD. A portrait head, to the left, which
has been attributed to C. Antius Restio. It has a signature, CKYΛAKO ; is a work deeply and finely cut, probably
by an Italian hand during the last century

> *Figured in the " Marlborough Gems," vol. ii. 8*

514 INTAGLIO ON CHALCEDONY. A laureated head to the right, of
Roman workmanship. In enamelled setting

> *An Arundel gem, perhaps rightly attributed to Geta in the
> Catalogue (Ar. Cat. Thec. A, No. 22). The work, however,
> seems too good for Geta's time*

515 INTAGLIO ON CORNELIAN. A bust to the right

516 INTAGLIO ON A GOLDEN SARD, to the right. A portrait head, the
hair finely worked ; of probably early Imperial date

> *Termed Marcus Agrippa in the Duke's Catalogue, but it is
> not like the great Admiral*

517 INTAGLIO ON A FINE SARD, to the left. A head, possibly meant
for Mæcenas. It is very bald, like the well-known portrait
signed " Solon "

> *An Arundel gem, termed in the Arundel Catalogue (Ar.
> Cat. Thec. A, 36), a head of Solon*

518 INTAGLIO ON A PALE SARD. Two conjugated Imperial heads, to the left, intended for an emperor and empress. The work is of the cinque-cento period

> *An Arundel gem (Ar. Cat. Thec. No. 14), called in the Catalogue Augustus and Livia*

519 INTAGLIO ON A NICOLO, to the left. A bearded head with a fillet

520 INTAGLIO ON A FINE YELLOW SARD, to the right. Portrait of a bearded personage, possibly of Clodius Albinus, worked in a remarkable manner, the hair falling in circular wreaths (calamus stratus ?). It is a Roman work

521 INTAGLIO ON A NICOLO, to the left. Portrait head, probably representing some Imperial prince in the character of Mercury; the caduceus behind his head, and a tortoise in the field

> *Figured in the " Marlborough Gems," vol. i. No. 5, and there denominated M. J. Brutus. It was purchased of a Mr. C. Morison for 60l.*

522 INTAGLIO ON A FINE RED SARD, a beardless head, to the left; attributed to Sulla. Finely worked, probably of cinque-cento age

> *One of the Arundel gems (Cat. Thec. A, No. 17)*
> *Figured in the " Marlborough Gems," vol. i. No. 2*

523 INTAGLIO ON CORNELIAN. Portrait bust, to the left, of a youthful personage, probably a son or nephew of one of the early Cæsars, perhaps Germanicus

524 INTAGLIO ON A SPLENDID SARD, three-quarter face, to the right. A cinque-cento bearded portrait

> *An Arundel gem (Cat. Thec. A, No. 26)*

525 INTAGLIO IN SARD. A portrait to the right, with a fillet, of cinque-cento date. Mounted as a seal

> *A Bessborough gem (Cat. No. 76)*

526 INTAGLIO ON A SARD, to the left. Helmeted bust. In enamelled gold ring set with two sapphires

*One of the Chesterfield gems (Cat. No. 17 c), and termed
by Natter Philip of Macedon*

Figured in Worlidge's Etchings

527 INTAGLIO ON A SARDONYX; a three-quarter faced bust, perhaps
meant for Demosthenes. It is cut in an upper layer of
yellow sard into a white layer, below which is another
stratum of yellow sard

528 CAMEO ON AN ONYX; bust, to the left. A minute work, the
head cut in considerable relief, in a white layer on a bluish-
grey ground

*A Bessborough gem (Cat. No. 94). Natter calls it Demo-
critus*

529 INTAGLIO ON A SARD. To the left, a finely cut bust portrait
set in a pretty ring

It was a Medina gem (Bess. Cat. No. 5 M)

530 CAMEO ON AN ONYX. A portrait head to the left, of small size,
but fine workmanship ; cut in a white layer on a bluish-grey
base. In finely enamelled gold ring

531 CAMEO ON A SARDONYX. Bust portrait to the right, with a
radiate crown of three rays; perhaps some Oriental prince,
under the Empire, at a late period. The paludamentum
and crown are in a brown layer, the face, hair, and neck of a
pinkish white supported by a white base layer. He is beardless, and wears an earring

An Arundel gem (Cat. Theo. B, No. 33)

532 CAMEO ON PALE-BLUE TURQUOISE, to the left. Portrait of an
unknown person, of fine workmanship, and apparently
antique

533 CAMEO, to the right. A bust of a bearded person, cut in a
translucent violet-tinted layer of an onyx, with a yellowish
base ; the hair and the drapery are left in a yellow upper
layer. In pierced mount set with stones ; the back chased

*Attributed by Natter, in the Bessborough Catalogue (No.
33 M), to Marcus Aurelius. It was one of the Medina gems*

534 A SMALL CAMEO ON AN ONYX; bust portrait, to the right, representing a warrior in a singular helmet; the helmet and part of the armour left in a white layer

An Arundel gem (Cat. Thec. A, No. 129)

535 CAMEO ON SARDONYX. A portrait of an ecclesiastic, to the right. It is a cinque-cento work of a very high character, in somewhat flat relief in a porcelain-white layer on a yellowish-brown base

An Arundel gem (Cat. Thec. B, No. 37)
See Illustration, p. 101

536 CAMEO ON AN ONYX. A three-quarter length representation of a negro, the drapery being left in a white layer, while the face and arm are represented in a stratum of black

An Arundel gem (Cat. Thec. A, No. 132)

537 CAMEO ON A FINE SARDONYX, $2\frac{3}{8}$ inches high, $1\frac{5}{8}$ inch wide. A bust portrait to the left of a helmeted warrior, the ægis and helmet left in a yellowish-brown layer, face in a whitish layer on a dark grey ground. It is a fine work of the cinquecento period

538 CAMEO ON AN ONYX, to the right. A very celebrated head, cut by Alessandro Cesati (Il Greco). It is not bearded, yet it has been called the portrait of Phocion; probably from a supposed similarity to the known gem with the inscription ΦΩΚΙΩΝΟΟ. That gem was pronounced by Vasari, in his life of A. Cesati, to be the *ne plus ultra* of the engraver's art. This cameo is $1\frac{3}{4}$ inch high by $1\frac{1}{2}$ inch wide, the face being cut in an opaque white layer. in rather shallow relief, on a reddish-brown base. It is splendidly mounted in a pierced and enamelled setting, forming a rich wreath of flowers, among which a sunflower recurs conspicuously

Figured in the "Marlborough Gems," vol. i. No. 28
This gem with the Horatius Cocles, No. 596, the Antinous, No. 501, and Matidia, probably the Sabina, No. 455, was bought by the third Duke for 600l. from Zanetti
See Illustration, p. 39

H

539 CAMEO ON SARDONYX. Small Imperial bust, to the right, in a whitish-blue layer on a dark-grey ground, the hair and a raised border showing a layer of yellow

> An Arundel gem (Cat. Thec. A, No. 113), called an Antinous

540 CAMEO ON ONYX; a negro's head, full-face. Renaissance work, in a dark upper layer on a white ground

> An Arundel gem (Cat. Thec. A, 126)

541 CAMEO ON ONYX; a heroic head, to the left. A very fine work, cut out of a flesh-coloured layer with a black base

> Figured as Caracalla in the " Marlborough Gems," vol. i. No. 23

542 CAMEO ON ONYX. Head, to the right, of an old man, wrinkled and bald. It is attributed to Caius Antius Restio whose portrait occurs on Consular coins when his son was a moneyer. Under truncation the letters M.D., signature of the engraver

543 CAMEO ON A CAT'S-EYE. A head of an unknown person, to the left

> A Bessborough gem (Cat. No. 91)

544 CAMEO ON AN ONYX. A portrait, to the left, cut in a white layer on a transparent ground

> A Bessborough gem (Cat. No. 18)
> Figured in the " Marlborough Gems," vol. i. No. 1, as Scipio Africanus

545 INTAGLIO ON A RED JASPER. Two heads, viz. those of a Roman lady and her child, apparently of the Antonine period

> An Arundel gem called in the Catalogue (Thec. A, No. 16), Agrippina and Drusus

546 INTAGLIO ON BROWN SARD. Two Roman (male and female) bust portraits, confronted; probably of private individuals of the age of Caracalla, the head-dress of the lady resembling that of Plautilla

> Probably an Arundel gem (in the Cat. Thec. A, No. 27)

547 INTAGLIO ON A SARD. Bust portraits, male and female, in
workmanship of the late Middle Empire. They may be
intended to represent Carinus and Magnia Urbica

*An Arundel gem, called in the Catalogue (Thec. A, No.
21) portraits of Antoninus Pius and Faustina*

548 INTAGLIO ON A SARD. Female head to the left. It seems to be
Roman work

An Arundel gem, termed Faustina (Cat. Thec. B, No. 28)

549 INTAGLIO ON AMETHYST; portrait of a lady to the left. A work
probably of the second century

An Arundel gem (Cat. Thec. A, No. 24), called Crispina

550 INTAGLIO HEAD ON A RED JASPER, to the left, of a lady with
head-dress similar to one of those among the Cyrene marbles
at the British Museum. Probably of the Antonine period

End of Third Day's Sale.

H 2

Fourth Day's Sale.

On THURSDAY, JUNE 29, 1899,

551 INTAGLIO ON A RED SARD. Portrait to the left, apparently of a Roman lady, mounted in a ring of extraordinary beauty, full-length figures forming either shank, while on the back of the bezel there are little birds

> One of the Chesterfield gems in the Bessborough Collection (Cat. No. 9 c), called Lucilla, and so figured in Worlidge's Etchings. Natter terms the stone a "Berill rouge"

552 INTAGLIO ON A FINE SARD. Bust to the left, apparently of a lady, but with a caduceus on the shoulder, whence it has been supposed to represent an Imperial youth, but the portrait is not that of any young Cæsar. It seems to be Roman work of about the Antonine period

553 INTAGLIO ON A SARD. A female head to the left

> A Bessborough gem (Cat. No. 26 c)

554 INTAGLIO ON A NICOLO, with brown base layer. Female head to the left

> From the Arundel Collection (Cat. Thec. A, No. 77)

555 INTAGLIO ON A NICOLO. Portrait, to the left

556 A SMALL CAMEO ON AN ONYX, cut in a red layer on a translucent white base, under which lies a blue stratum. It represents a female head, to the left. Mounted as a pendant

557 CAMEO ON A SPLENDID SARDONYX, of 1¾ inch in length, by 1 inch in width. Portrait, to the left, veiled, with a sceptre, probably of an empress. It may represent Julia Mæsa, and certainly does not seem earlier than the time of Elagabalus The face and a reserved rim are in white, the hair and the veil are in a rich brown layer, the robe in one of a paler hue of brown. In metal-gilt frame set with two rubies (?) and an amethyst

One of the Arundel gems (Cat. Thec. D, No. 1), called Julia Mæsa

559 CAMEO ON SARDONYX. Female head, to the right; the face in a white opaque layer. The abundant and boldly worked hair left in a yellow tint, the base being black. It is a beautiful work

560 CAMEO ON ONYX. Small female head, to the right; cut in a porcelain-white layer on a dark-grey ground. It is antique in character

561 CAMEO ON SARDONYX. Portrait, to the right; bust of a lady in a head-dress of the fashion of the time of Titus. The reserved rim and head are cut in a brown layer on a white ground. It is shallow work, well finished, and probably cinque-cento in date

An Arundel gem (Cat. Thec. B, No. 8)

562 CAMEO ON A SARD. Portrait of a lady to the right, in a dress of the early sixteenth century; the face being apparently artificially whitened, or possibly cut on a white mark in the stone

An Arundel gem (Cat. Thec. B, No. 10), called Sappho

563 CAMEO ON ONYX. Bust portrait of a lady to the right. Cut in a white stratum on a grey base

Perhaps an Arundel gem called a Livia (Cat. Thec. B, No. 14)

564 CAMEO ON AN ONYX. Veiled bust portrait, to the right, of a lady, cut in a white stratum on one of pinkish grey

An Arundel gem (Ar. Cat. Thec. D, No. 6)

565 CAMEO ON A SARDONYX.   Portrait, to the left, of a lady, cut in
a white layer, with a base of dark sard.   The beautiful
setting is formed of a hollow wreath of flowers exquisitely
enamelled in colours, the back being adorned with deep blue
enamel and black arabesque work
See Illustration, p. 39

566 CAMEO ON A MAGNIFICENT ONYX, 3 inches by 1⅞ inch.   A lady
in a veil, represented by a bust portrait to the left; the
design, in an oval form, being supported by an acanthus
flower.   It is very beautiful work, the figure and a reserved
rim cut in flat relief out of a rich dark-brown layer with a
base of white.   It is by some admirable cinque-cento artist.
In gold frame
An Arundel gem (Cat. Thec. D, No. 4)

567 CAMEO ON A SARDONYX.   Bust, to the right, of a lady.   A pretty
cinque-cento work, in a white upper layer of the stone, with
a transparent yellow base layer
An Arundel gem (Cat. Thec. A, No. 130)

568 CAMEO ON AN ONYX   A head, to the right.   Portrait of a
lady

569 CAMEO ON AN ONYX.   Portrait, to the left, much undercut; it
is a good work of the cinque-cento period

570 CAMEO ON ONYX.   Two conjugated and helmeted female heads,
to the right; perhaps representing deities.   The helmets, of
each are left in a pale red stratum, the faces and ground
being white

571 CAMEO ON JASPER ONYX.   Three-quarter face and bust of a
negress; an asp inflicting a wound on her bosom.   It is a
Renaissance work, cut in a layer of black jasper, on a sard
base.   The stone is bevelled off all round, and is of the
dimensions of 2¼ inches in height and 1¾ inch in width.   In
gold enamelled mount, the back decorated with scroll work

*A Bessborough gem, termed Cleopatra, for whom, doubtless,
the Renaissance artist intended the African features (Cat.
No. 16)*

572 A Cameo on an Onyx. Being a head and bust, to the left, in a white layer on a base of an amethyst tint

An Arundel gem (Ar. Cat. Thec. B, No. 9), called a head of Berenice

573 Cameo on Onyx. A female head, to the right, cut in a white layer on a black ground

One of the Bessborough gems (Cat. No. 77)

574 Cameo on Onyx, white upon black ground. A portrait of a lady, to the right

575 Cameo on an Onyx. Head of a lady, to the right, in a white layer, on bluish grey. On the back is an intaglio: figures of a lady and a boy, bezel of ring set with brilliants

Probably an Arundel gem (Cat. Thec. B, No. 13)

576 Cameo on a Pretty Sardonyx, with a female head, to the left, wearing a sort of mural crown. A bevelled rim left round the head, exhibiting a yellow layer besides the brownish layer in which the head is cut, in flat relief with a white ground

Perhaps an Arundel gem (Cat. Thec. B, No. 28)

577 Cameo on Onyx. A female head

578 Cameo in very Flat Relief on a Sardonyx, of the finest quality; 2¼ inches in length, 1¾ inch in width. It is a bust portrait to the right, in a bluish layer on a black ground, traces of a brown surface layer being left in the hair and robe. Mounted in a gold enamelled border with loop

An Arundel gem (Cat. Thec. D, No. 10) termed Junia Claudia

579 Cameo on Sardonyx, 2¼ inches in length by 1 inch in breadth. Portrait of a lady, in one-third length figure, turning her back, face looking to the right, in a white translucent layer on a dark ground. It is mounted in a rococo openwork setting of the time of Louis XV., carrying enamelled trophies, and ten small sardonyxes and onyxes.

Probably an Arundel gem, termed Cleopatra (Ar. Cat. Thec. D, No. 5)

See Illustration, p. 106

580 A LARGE CAMEO ON AN ONYX, with two different layers of
pinkish white; 2 inches by 1 inch in dimensions, representing a female head

*Probably an Arundel gem, termed Octavia (Ar. Cat. Thec.
B, No. 6)*

581 CAMEO ON ONYX. A negress head in front face.   A Renaissance work, cut in a brown layer on a bluish-white base

582 INTAGLIO ON A CHALCEDONY. Head to the right, by Marchant
—*signed*. A beautiful and elaborate work, recorded in the
handwriting of the third Duke of Marlborough as being a
copy from a work by Fiamingo; a head of Susannah

(4.) *PORTRAITURE OF MODERN PERSONAGES.*

583 INTAGLIO ON A SPINEL-RUBY. A deeply cut minute head in
front face, wearing a coronet with fleurs-de-lis. It is set in a
contemporary gold ring, with the words "Tel il nest"—
"There is none such as he," inscribed on a ring

This most interesting and minute intaglio is in all probability the identical signet of Charles V. of France, described
in the inventory of his valuables, made in 1379 : "Le signet
du Roy qui est de la teste d'un roy sans barbe; et est d'un
fin rubis d'Orient : c'est celui de quoi le roy scelle les lettres
qu'il escript de sa main." It accords exactly with the head
surmounting the royal figure on his coins; and it is a most
interesting gem, as illustrating the skill of the gem engraver
at so early an age as the fourteenth century

*An Arundel gem (Cat. Thec. A, No. 27) termed in the Cata-
logue a Lombard king*

584 CAMEO ON A SARDONYX. A minute portrait to the right, of
Philip II. of Spain, cut in a shallow manner in a white layer
on a dark-grey ground, with traces of an upper yellow layer
on the hair and collar

An Arundel gem (Cat. Thec A, No. 128)

No. 535.

No. 590.

No. 275.

No. 586.

No. 499.

No. 145.

585 CAMEO ON AN ONYX. Portrait to the left. The hair in a yellowish layer, face in one of whitish blue, on ground of bluish grey. It is early Renaissance work, representing apparently some personage of that period, perhaps Cosmo de Medici; called, however, in the Arundel Catalogue (Thec. A, No. 104), Clodius Albinus. In chased gold ring

586 CAMEO ON A FINE SARDONYX. Portrait, to the right, of Philip II., apparently by Jacopo da Trezzo. It is beautifully cut in a clear white layer, with a base of sard; at the back is an eagle standing on a serpent, a mountainous country behind, a motto engraved round it, "Nihil est quod non tolleret qui perfectè diligit."

A gem from the Bessborough Collection (Cat. No. 12)
See Illustration

587 CAMEO ON CRYSTAL. Portrait of Philip II., to the left in armour. It is cut in rather low relief by an admirable hand; it bears on the pauldon·A·F·, the signature of the artist. In enamelled gold border

An Arundel gem (Cat. Thec. B, No. 35)

588 A SMALL CAMEO ON A SAPPHIRE, representing Henry IV. of France; without doubt a contemporary work

A Bessborough gem, termed Gustavus Adolphus (Cat. No. 89)

589 CAMEO ON ONYX. A contemporary portrait, to the left, of Mary Queen of Scots. It is in rather high relief, and is mounted in the original blue enamel gold locket: it is cut in a white layer with a grey base

590 CAMEO ON SARDONYX. Portrait, with bust, to the right, of Cardinal Mazarin, boldly cut, though in low relief, in a yellow layer on a light mottled ground. Contemporary work

A Bessborough gem (Cat. No. 11)
See Illustration

591 CAMEO ON A SARD. A bust portrait, to the left, in low relief, probably representing Diana of Poitiers, carrying a quiver behind her. The reverse is an intaglio Venus and Cupid.

An Arundel gem (Cat. Thec. B, No. 22)
See Illustration, p. 48

592 CAMEO ON A SARDONYX. A portrait to the right, in rather high
relief and fine execution, of a lady, supposed by Mr. Way to
be Lady Alathea Talbot, wife of Lord Arundel. It is surrounded by a setting of enamelled gold, with ten garnets engraved with clasped hands; having been probably a wedding
gift. The hair and the drapery are worked in two different
shades of red, the face in a white layer, while the ground is
black. A third red layer, elsewhere cut away, is employed
for the left shoulder. On the back is enamelled a gold
tressure on a blue ground

It was an Arundel gem (Cat. Thec. C, No. 8)

593 AN INTAGLIO ON YELLOW QUARTZ. Small contemporary portrait
to the right of James II. Set as a seal

A Bessborough gem (Cat. No. 84)

III. SUBJECTS FROM HISTORY AND DAILY LIFE, &c.

(1.) *HISTORICAL SUBJECTS.*

594 INTAGLIO ON A LARGE STRIPED AGATE. The allocution of
Pescennius Niger; who is represented addressing the Syrian
Legions, and in the act of landing. It is a cinque-cento
work, set so as to be worn as a medallion; an octahedron
of spinel adorns the ring for suspension

An Arundel gem (Cat. Thec. E, No. 19)

595 CAMEO ON AN ONYX, representing Horatius Cocles defending
the bridge. A marvel of cinque-cento work, on account of
the multitude of figures and the minuteness with which they
are delineated. Mars is represented appearing in clouds,
and together with the bridge and exaggerated figures upon
it, he is rendered in a white layer, on a base of grey. In
gold mount with enamelled edge

An Arundel gem (Cat. Thec. B, No. 42)

596 CAMEO ON AN ONYX. Same subject as the last, but finished still more minutely. The hero is represented on horseback, and he and the other figures are not less heroic in proportions than in No. 595

See Illustration, p. 48

(2.) *DIVINATION, SACRIFICES, &c.*

597 INTAGLIO ON A LARGE SARD, an inch in length. A full-length figure seated, and holding downwards a twig or wand, perhaps an augur taking the auspices

598 INTAGLIO ON A PALE GARNET. A priestess going to a sacrifice raising an incense vessel before her: a lighted torch in the field perhaps indicates, as Mr. King has suggested, the nocturnal character of the Dionysian rites. Very fine Roman work

An Arundel gem (Cat. Thec. A, No. 78)

599 CAMEO ON LAPIS LAZULI. Veiled female bust to the left, somewhat like the Philistis on the coins of Syracuse, called by Natter a Sibyl

From the Bessborough Collection (Cat. No. 29)

600 INTAGLIO ON A PALE PLASMA. A representation of a sacrifice; a man, carrying the implements of sacrifice on his head, drags a goat towards a little altar, on which a woman drops incense, behind her a Satyr plays the double pipes. It exhibits the elegant drawing characteristic of the work on this stone, which was so much in use after the middle of the first century

601 INTAGLIO ON A HYCINTHINE GARNET. A simple female figure carrying a plate of fruit in her left hand, and a small cantharus in her right, proceeds to a sacrifice. An elegant work, by one of the masters of the last century

602 A SMALL CAMEO ON SARDONYX, representing a sacrifice to
Jupiter, offered apparently by a bearded Bacchus, and Pan,
Apollo, and two female personages. A well engraved and
curious little work of the cinque-cento time, in a white layer
on a translucent red base. In openwork setting with sapphires and diamonds

It was one of the Medina gems (Bess. Cat. No. 35 x)

603 CAMEO ON SARDONYX. A woman going to a nocturnal sacrifice ;
a little girl precedes her carrying a flambeau in one hand
and an œnochoë in the other. It is cut in a white ivory
layer on a base of brown. The work, particularly the drapery,
is excellent, and belongs to an early period of Imperial
Rome

An Arundel gem (Cat. Thec. B, No. 46)

Figured in the "Marlborough Gems," vol. i. No. 43

(3.) WAR.

604 INTAGLIO ON A CORNELIAN. The arms of a warrior, including
the sword, greaves, and helmet, hung on a date palm ; a ram,
representing perhaps Aries as a horoscope, is under the tree ;
over it the letters MEANDER, Meander, or perhaps Menander,
in ligature ; doubtless the name of the owner. The work is
delicate, and probably of an early Imperial date. Mr. King
suggests that this gem may refer to the defeat by Lucullus of
Menander, the general of Mithridates. It would seem with
more probability to represent the dedication by a Gladiator
of his arms and accoutrements after an agonistic victory.

One of the Bessborough gems (Cat. No. 68)

605 INTAGLIO ON A NICOLO. A combat between a warrior and an
amazon. Roman work

One of the Chesterfield gems (Bessb. Cat. No. 33 c)

606 INTAGLIO ON A YELLOW SARD. A Thessalian horseman, distinguished by his hat. The horse has the sash of victory (tonia) depending from his head. The drawing is spirited, it is probably by a late Greek artist. The figure recalls one on coins of Larissa and on those of Alexander of Pheræ

607 INTAGLIO ON A PALE GREEN PLASMA. A fallen archer is extracting a spear from his side, while he holds in his right hand a bow. Another warrior is defending him with spear and shield. The work is in fine shallow engraving in the Greek style; but the form of the shield is Roman, and the work belongs, probably, to the early Imperial times, when the plasma was beginning to come into vogue

Figured in the " Marlborough Gems," vol. i. No. 42

608 INTAGLIO ON A SARD, about 1¼ inch in height by ⅝ths of an inch in width. A warrior, nude, with his shield and armour by his side, stands in front of a horse, whose bridle he holds. Probably Greek work. Mounted as a seal

It was in the Arundel Collection (Ar. Cat. Thec. E, No. 16)
Figured as Alexander and Bucephalus in the " Marlborough Gems," vol. i. No. 45

609 INTAGIO ON A SARD. Three warriors (the Horatii) in three-quarter length busts, full-faced ; one of them carries a shield with a gryphon killing a deer for a cognisance : the central figure has upon his breast-plate a head, perhaps of Medusa. It is good Roman work, deeply sunk

Figured in the " Marlborough Gems," vol. i. No. 41
Purchased by the third Duke

610 INTAGLIO ON A SARD. A warrior on horseback, guided by Pallas. A late Roman work

611 INTAGLIO ON A NICOLO. A galley. Both the subject and the treatment are late Roman in character

612 INTAGLIO ON A FINE SARDONYX, with a thick upper layer of sard, and an under layer of transparent bluish chalcedony. It represents a full-length nude figure, with the left arm extended, and the right drawn back to the ear, as if in the act of pulling an arrow, or perhaps a boxer about to deliver a blow; in the latter case it may represent Pollux. The head is somewhat after the type of Hercules. The gem is set in a beautiful enamelled mounting, with a white ground and coloured flowers, *temp.* Louis XIII. The work is fine

An Arundel gem (Cat. Thec. E, No. 6)

613 INTAGLIO ON A FINE SARDONYX, with a rich brown upper layer on a white base, and a narrow intermediate yellowish layer. The same singular subject as the last

614 INTAGLIO ON A LARGE CONVEX SARDONYX, with deep brown upper layer passing into a white under layer, representing a Greek horseman, with lance and circular buckler, riding at full speed

615 A LARGE CAMEO ON ONYX, cut in an opaque white layer, and representing a warrior in bust to the left, with helmet and armour most elaborately ornamented. It is undercut, and in very high relief. In an open gold setting of scroll design, with emeralds, sapphires, &c.

This gem came into the Bessborough Cabinet from the Medina Collection. It had before been in that of Lord Halifax. It passed for King Pyrrhus (Bessb. Cat. No. 38 M) Figured in the " Marlborough Gems," vol. ii. No. 7 See Illustration

616 CAMEO ON A SMALL ONYX, representing a cavalry combat; one standard having the letters S·P·Q·R. An elaborate little gem of the cinque-cento time

617 AN INTAGLIO ON A LARGE YELLOW PASTE. A Roman warrior riding down a foe. It is a subject frequent as a reverse on Imperial Roman coins, from Trajan to Probus, or even to Constantine

From the Molinari Cabinet

No. 615.

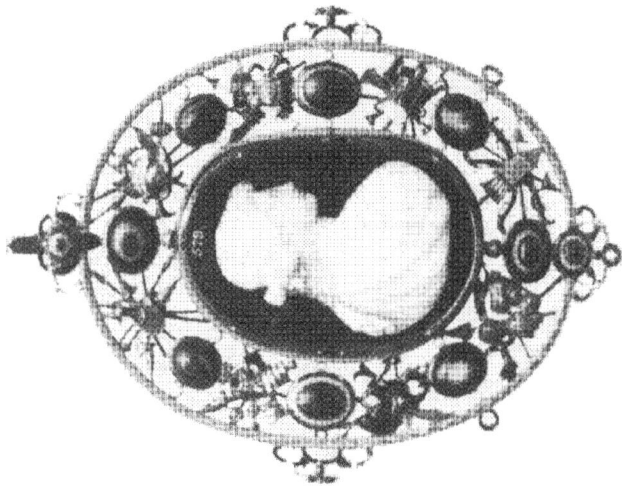

No. 579.

618 Intaglio on a Thin Yellow Sard, with a white rim reserved round it, or afterwards cemented on. It is a little microscopic subject of a warrior and a female shaking hands. It is scratched in with the point, and carries the signature L. S. of Louis Siriès, a French engraver of the last century

619 Intaglio on a Fine Banded Agate. Four figures; a man who is seated receives a person, behind whom stand two warriors. The work is in every way worthy of a master hand

620 Intaglio on a Yellow Paste. A triumphal procession

620a Cameo on Onyx; a minute gem, on which a bearded warrior stands between two female personages. On one hand is a trophy, on the other a youth sacrifices at an altar. It is probably a Roman work, referring to a victory. In enamelled gold ring

An Arundel gem (Cat. Thec. A, No. 134)

620b Fragment of a Large Cameo on Sardonyx. On the ground is a prostrate barbarian female figure, in an attitude of grief; another figure seems as though blowing a trumpet, while a horse bears a large German shield. The work is extremely fine, perhaps part of a subject representing the triumph of Drusus. The mourning figure, the herald and the horse are rendered in a fine white layer, the rest in a pale brownish sard layer

This was an Arundel gem (Ar. Cat. B, No. 47)

Figured in the " Marlborough Gems," vol. i. No. 47

(4.) *THE GAMES. THE THEATRE.*

621 INTAGLIO ON A FINE HYACINTHINE SARDINE. An athlete with the lettering : ∵ :: .⁚. : OY, which may be read either as ΓΝΑΙΟΥ or ΓΗΑΙΟΥ : but the letters have been polished away till only the points remain. In the field is a tripod with a jar. It has been described as an athlete anointing himself. It may, however, be a representation of the subject of the Diadumenos of Polycletus, of which the statue in the British Museum is supposed to be a copy, and which represents an athlete binding a diadem round his head. Natter in his Catalogue calls it " un Berill d'une beauté achevée " (see No. 43)

> *It was from the Bessborough Collection (Cat. No. 36), and was formerly the property of Clement V., and afterwards successively in the cabinets of Apostolo Zeno and of Stosch*
>
> *Figured in the " Marlborough Gems," vol. i. No. 35, where the stone is described as a hyacinthine Sardine approaching the Hyacinth, called by the Italians Giacinto Guarnacino*

621a INTAGLIO ON A YELLOWISH SARD. A copy of the last, possibly by Natter's inimitable hand, even to the polished down character of the surface and the lettering of the name being precisely copied. This gem is an admirable illustration of the way in which antique gems could be copied in the last century

621b TWO PASTE CAMEOS BY MARCHANT, in white on black, on an onyx ; also an admirable copy from the famous gem described in 621

622 INTAGLIO ON A VERY FINE RUBY SARD, nearly circular in form. A Discobolus with all the appearance of being good Greek work. The circular form of the gem may be itself in allusion to that of the disc

> *One of the Medina gems (Bessb. Cat. No. 2 M)*
> *Figured among Worlidge's Etchings*

623 INTAGLIO ON AN OBLONG SARD, slightly convex. A Discobolus, somewhat lengthy in the drawing ; an early Roman work of Imperial time. Set in a finely enamelled seal, adorned with fleurs-de-lis

624 INTAGLIO ON A RED SARD, with a " chevron "-formed streak across it. A horse stands with a youth by him who reins him in. It is enclosed in the " Etruscan " border, and is rendered in the shallow manner and with the delicate *technique* of the early Greek style, while also the rein of the horse carries the bosses characteristic of the Greek bridle

One of the Arundel gems (Cat. Thec. A, No. 63)

Figured among the Etchings of Worlidge

625 INTAGLIO ON A CORNELIAN. A small quadriga of Roman workmanship

A Bessborough gem (Cat. No. 45)

626 INTAGLIO ON A BANDED AGATE. An actor in front of a mask on a Term, studying his part. It is Greco-Roman work

A Bessborough gem (Cat. No. 62)

627 INTAGLIO ON A VERY FINE OBLONG CONVEX SARD. A figure, apparently of a comic actor carrying the hooked cane, his attribute. It is spiritedly drawn, and rather deeply cut ; probably rather late Greek work. A gem in the Payne Knight Collection, British Museum, represents a similar subject

From the Medina Collection (Bessb. Cat. No. 9 M)

(5.) *DOMESTIC AND PASTORAL OCCUPATIONS.*

628 An Intaglio Copy on Cornelian, of the famous signet of Michael Angelo, by Gio. Maria da Pescia, in the Bibliothèque Impériale at Paris

629 Intaglio on a Sard. A sculptor chiselling a bust; a star in the field, and also a Term with a palm branch, a wreath and a vase. Perhaps a prize to a successful competitor, Greek or Greco-Roman work. At the back is the symbolic word IXΘYC directly written

A Bessborough gem (Cat. No. 51)

630 Intaglio on a Little Nicolo, representing two persons, perhaps children, rolling two large discs along the ground like the modern Italian nuzzuoli. It is good Roman work

631 Intaglio on a Fine Nicolo. A poulterer carrying on a pole over his shoulders a rabbit and a cock. A nice Roman gem

632 Intaglio on a Very Fine Nicolo. Huntsman accompanied by a dog, carrying a rabbit on a pole. Late Roman work

633 Intaglio on a Nicolo. Herdsman driving a cow. Roman work

One of the Medina gems, termed by Natter Argus watching Io (Bessb. Cat. No. 8 м)

634 Intaglio on a Nicolo. A herdsman yoking a bull, having put a ladder against the animal in order to raise the yoke. Roman work

635 Cameo or "Intaglio Rilevato"; a very large oval bloodstone, on which a girl is represented in the manner of Egyptian cameo or carvesque work, as though balancing the astragalus

636 Cameo on an Onyx. A work of the late Renaissance period, in which a male and female figure are represented; the former seated, the latter apparently coming to him for protection. The figures and reserved rim are worked in a brown layer

Arundel gem (Cat. Thec. C, No. 20)

637 Intaglio on a Sard. A Spinthriate subject

One of the Medina gems (Cat. No. 11 м)

(6.) *URNS, SOUVENIRS, &c.*

638 INTAGLIO ON A SARD. An urn with a basket-work pattern, and two handles formed as of the head and neck of a bird. Roman work

An Arundel gem (Cat. Thec. A, No. 72)

639 INTAGLIO ON A FINE NICOLO. A vase; by Marchant

640 INTAGLIO ON A SARD. Female head to the left, in a head-dress of the latter part of the second century; worked, with the direct inscription ΕΥΠΟΡ ΑΙΑ ΠѠΤΙΑ, " May you ever prosper, Potia "

641 INTAGLIO ON A BLOODSTONE. A hand holding out a dead mouse. Work of the second century

642 CAMEO ON AN ONYX; with a device of the hand pinching an ear, and the direct circumscription ΜΝΗΜΟΝΕΥΕ. The device is left in a white layer on a black ground. It is a Roman work

One of the Medina gems (Cat. No. 18 M)

643 CAMEO ON AN ONYX. A hand twitching an ear, " aurem vellit," with the direct superscription ΜΝΗΜΟΝΕΥΕ ΜΟΥ ΤΗС ΚΑΛΗС ΨΥΧΗС ΕΥΤΥΧΙ СѠΦΡΟΝΙ: " Remember me, your pretty love, good luck to you, Sophronios: " being a souvenir from a lady. Between the device and the lettering there runs a curious thong, as if articulated, with four knots; perhaps, as Mr. King suggests, the " Heracleus nodus," symbol of wedlock. The gem is cut in extremely flat relief and recalls in its manner the early Byzantine work. It is probably of the fourth century. The device is cut in a thin greenish layer, supported by a horny understratum

644 CAMEO, with an inscription, cut directly in a thin white layer of an onyx, with a black base. ΕΥΤΥΧΙ ΒΕΡΟΝΙΚΗ: " May you prosper, O Beronice " (or Veronica). Roman work

I 2

IV. CHRISTIAN AND MEDIÆVAL SUBJECTS.

645 INTAGLIO ON A FINE BOHEMIAN GARNET, cut *en cabochon*, representing St. Michael and Lucifer. It is a fine work of the Renaissance period

One of the Arundel gems (Cat. Thec. C, No. 23)

646 CAMEO ON AN ONYX. The Madonna of the Assumption standing on the head of a winged angel, four similar angels' heads being arranged on each side of her; the Madonna's hands are clasped. Cut in a white layer in rather high relief on a bluish base. It is a work of the Renaissance, mounted in a rich gold setting of a vine stem carrying vine leaves

One of the Arundel gems (Cat. Thec. C, No. 24)

647 A MINUTE CAMEO. A head cut in a white layer on a red base. An early Renaissance work, described by Natter as John the Baptist

From the Bessborough Collection (Cat. No. 88)

648 THREE FIGURES OF SAINTS, worked on a sard, the forms being left in the original colour of the stone, the rest being wrought in white by the action of an alkali on the surface. The figures have tints imparted to them by colours painted under the translucent stone. It was a fanciful mode of working in the sixteenth century

649 A REPRESENTATION, by a similar treatment of the surface of a red sard, of the entry of Christ into Jerusalem. It is a good composition with many figures

650 A SHELL CAMEO, slightly convex, representing the Three Kings (of Cologne); cut in pink layers of a shell. It is work of cinque-cento time. One of the heads is represented in darker layers than the rest, as representing Africa, and contrasted with the others representing Europe and Asia

A Bessborough gem (Cat. No. 79)

V. MASKS, CAPRICES AND ANIMAL FORMS.

(1.) *MASKS.*

651 INTAGLIO ON A CORNELIAN. Three-quarter face comic mask, with the name KVINTIL. The name seems genuine, and probably recalls the Roman owner of the gem
A Bessborough gem (Cat. No. 39)

652 INTAGLIO ON A BRIGHT-RED JASPER. Tragic and comic masks conjoined. A fine Roman work
A Bessborough gem (Cat. No. 41)

653 INTAGLIO ON A MOST EXCELLENT NICOLO. A comic bearded mask of fine and early workmanship
A Bessborough gem (Cat. No. 63)

654 INTAGLIO ON A GOOD NICOLO. A Satyric mask with the lettering ΛΟΥΚΤΕΙ. The lettering is certainly genuine. It is a fine antique work, and was formerly in the Collection of Gorlæus: vide Dactyl. No. 506
A Bessborough gem (Cat. No. 65)

655 INTAGLIO ON A SARD. A full-faced mask of a Davus, or comic slave (the Buffoon). An excellent early Imperial work
A Bessborough gem (Cat. No. 64)

656 INTAGLIO ON A SARD. A Silenus mask in front face. Very fine work of early Imperial days
One of the Chesterfield gems, termed by Natter a bust of Plato (Cat. No. 22 c)

657 INTAGLIO ON A MOTTLED CHALCEDONY. Small comic mask, perhaps representing the "old man" (the *iratus Chremes*, as Mr. King suggests). Spirited early Roman work
One of the Medina gems (Cat. No. 6 M, termed a Nicolo)

658 INTAGLIO ON A NICOLO. A small comic mask. Roman work
   A Medina gem (Cat. No. 26 M)

659 INTAGLIO ON A NICOLO. A comic mask, of the time of the third
   century

660 INTAGLIO ON A SARD. Two masks representing Socrates and
   Xantippe confronted. A very clever and minute work of
   the best Roman period
   A Medina gem (Bessb. Cat. No. 17 M)

661 INTAGLIO ON A SARD. Two masks conjoined; a Roman work.
   A Medina gem (Cat. No. 15 M)

662 INTAGLIO ON A SPLENDID BLOOD SARD. A beautiful caprice,
   representing a female head conjoined with two Silenus
   masks. Extremely fine Roman work
   One of the Arundel gems (Cat. Thec. A, No. 6)

663 INTAGLIO ON GOLDEN SARD. A very beautiful mask of the
   Bearded Bacchus. Fine and somewhat early Greek work-
   manship
   An Arundel gem (Cat. Thec. A, No. 65)

664 INTAGLIO ON A FINE SARD. Three masks, resembling heads of
   Hercules, Apollo, and Bacchus, with the pedum beneath
   them. Fi n early Roman work, set in a ring beautifully
   enamelled in black
   An Arundel gem (Cat. Thec. A, No. 4)

665 INTAGLIO ON A RED SARD. A deeply cut mask of a Cyclops,
   highly vigorous in its expression. Probably Roman work of
   the best Imperial time
   Figured among Worlidge's Etchings

666 INTAGLIO ON A JASPER. A mask and a wild boar's head conjugated opposite ways. Under them are written the letters
   ΘΙΕ, perhaps a play on a word of which the design forms
   part

667 INTAGLIO ON A MINUTE CABOCHON GARNET. An "aged" mask

668 INTAGLIO ON A BANDED AGATE CUT EN CABOCHON. It is a tragic
   mask of fine Roman workmanship

669 INTAGLIO ON A YELLOW SARD. A mask like a clown's head, with the mouth formed of a scallop shell: probably representing a fountain

670 CAMEO ON A SPLENDID BLOOD-RED SARD. A fine mask, nearly full-face ; probably antique

671 INTAGLIO ON A BANDED AGATE, with a group of four masks and the name HELENA across the gem
A Bessborough gem (Cat. No. 3 o)

672 INTAGLIO ON A MOTTLED GREEN AND YELLOW JASPER. Three conjoined masks
One of the Chesterfield gems (Cat. No. 44 o)

673 CAMEO ON A SARD. A Satyric mask in high relief
A Bessborough gem. Natter (Cat. No. 38) suggests that the eyes were once represented in metal ; or more probably, they contained precious stones that have been removed

674 CAMEO ON A YELLOW SARD. A comic mask of second century workmanship
A Bessborough gem (Cat. No. 40)

675 CAMEO ON A WHITE ONYX. A small comic mask, probably of Roman workmanship

676 A MINUTE CAMEO ON ONYX, representing a spirited little mask rendered in a red stratum ; the beard being done in a white layer on a dark ground
One of the Medina gems (Cat. No. 24 M)

677 CAMEO ON SARDONYX. A mask cut on a red stratum, the beard being rendered in a white layer on a dark ground, into which the eyes and mouth are cut down. A ever Roman work
A Medina gem (Cat. No. 26 M)

678 CAMEO ON AN ONYX. A Bacchic mask, in which the crown of the head is fractured. An antique work in a white layer on a yellowish base

679 CAMEO ON A CHERT-LIKE JASPER, 1 inch by ⅞; a stone that occasionally occurs with fine antique work. A front-faced Bacchic mask, in rather low relief. It is a spirited and undoubtedly antique work

680 CAMEO ON AN ONYX. A mask as of a youthful Bacchus; over each brow a little spot of red cornelian represents the corymbi. It is a Roman work, cut in a white layer on a red cornelian base

681 CAMEO ON AN ONYX. Silenus mask, in front-face: a head bound with a fillet with two corymbi. It is an excellent Roman work in flat relief, cut in a white layer on a dark-grey base

682 CAMEO ON AN ONYX. A mask in very high relief

683 CAMEO. A front-face mask. In gold frame with loop

(2.) GRYLLI, CAPRICES, &c.

684 INTAGLIO ON A NICOLO. A gryllus, representing a bald Silenus head united at the back with a goat's head. A good Roman work

> One of the Bessborough gems (Cat. No. 67)

685 INTAGLIO ON JASPER, beautifully set. A caprice, in which a Cupid rides a horse, of which only the head and neck are equine, the body being formed of a ram's head eating an ear of corn; the chest is formed by a mask with a projection from the chin, which supports a goat that is disputing with the horse for a wisp of hay; below it is a serpent. The lower part of the design is formed of an eagle tearing a hare, as on the coins of Agrigentum

> This elaborate caprice was one of the Chesterfield gems (Cat. No. 36 c)

686 INTAGLIO ON A SPLENDID BLOOD SARD. A gryllus, in which a peacock and a ram's head are combined with an elephant's head, a serpent, and a Silenus mask. Round it are the letters, ANICE. T. P. S. Work of late Roman time
One of the Medina gems (Cat. No. 12 M). It was published by Berioni at Rome

687 INTAGLIO ON A JASPER, carrying a gryllus representing a horse's head and neck, a mask, &c., on cocks' legs. Roman work
An Arundel gem (Cat. Thec. A, No. 34)

688 INTAGLIO ON A FINE NICOLO. A gryllus representing an elephant's head ingeniously combined with two masks. A pretty caprice of very nice Roman work
An Arundel gem (Cat. Thec. A, No. 66)

689 INTAGLIO ON A CORNELIAN. A goat, a horse, and a boar united to form a gryllus. A good example of Roman work

690 INTAGLIO ON A BERYL. A head of Jupiter, perhaps, of Jupiter Ammon, united to a ram's head, and with a curved neck over it somewhat like the Egyptian Vulture head-dress; in the beak of the bird's head is a small branch, perhaps of olive. The whole caprice is borne upon a pair of cock's legs. A work of a good period

691 INTAGLIO ON A SARD. A Siren: a beautifully cut gem
One of the Bessborough gems (Cat. No. 108)

(3.) *ANIMAL FORMS.*

692 INTAGLIO ON A SARD. A ram, or Aries as an astronomical symbol, the fleece being burnt white by an artificial process. It is Roman work

693 INTAGLIO ON AN ONYX, cut *en cabochon*. A goat browsing on a large ear of corn is engraved in the top layer, of a coral-red colour. The work is of the ordinary Roman type

694 CAMEO ON A VERY SMALL ONYX OF TWO GOATS, cut in an upper white layer

 One of the Bessborough gems (Cat. No. 49)

695 INTAGLIO ON A YELLOWISH SARD. A sow : very good work by Marchant

696 INTAGLIO ON A BANDED SARD. A bull ; a crescent in the field. A nicely executed Roman gem, set in a most handsome ring of the last century, ornamented with twisted vines

 An Arundel gem (Cat. Thec. A, No. 84)

697 INTAGLIO ON A GOOD SARD. A bull, represented, by a Roman artist, in the position of the bull on the coins of Thurium

698 INTAGLIO ON A FINE GOLDEN SARD. Four cows ; three are standing and one lying down. The gem has the appearance of a work by a good Roman artist

 An Arundel gem (Cat. Thec. A, No. 70)

699 INTAGLIO ON A TRANSPARENT CHALCEDONY. A cow, in late Roman work. Mounted as a seal

 Perhaps the Arundel gem (Cat. Thec. A, 69)

700 INTAGLIO ON A SARD. A cow and calf, of good antique workmanship

701 INTAGLIO ON A CORNELIAN. A horse or ass

 Possibly the Arundel gem (Cat. Thec. A, No. 98)

702 CAMEO ON AN ONYX, slightly convex. Two horses ; one drinks and the other stands by him. The forms are drawn in beautiful proportion, and it is a work probably by a Greek hand and of high merit

 One of the Arundel gems (Cat. Thec. A, No. 135)

703 A GLASS PASTE COPY OF THE ABOVE

704 CAMEO IN AN ONYX. A chestnut horse, represented in his natural colour in an upper layer of the stone, on a dark base layer. The horse is biting at a fetter. A work, from the treatment of its anatomical detail, attributable to the second century

705 CAMEO ON AN ONYX. An elephant trampling on a long and large fish, which he is goring with his tusks. It is a work remarkable for its spirited character and correct design. Mr. King has ingeniously suggested that it alludes to the fabled combats between elephants and monstrous eels in Indian rivers, recorded by Ctesias

706 CAMEO ON SARDONYX. An animal, perhaps a lynx, cut in a white layer on a brownish-red base. Very nice early antique work
Arundel gem (Ar. Cat. Thec. A, 143)

707 CAMEO, of a poodle or lap dog. Perhaps Roman

708 A CAMEO, apparently representing two dogs wearing comic masks, and probably a Roman work

709 INTAGLIO ON A NICOLO, representing a fox, in Roman work. Mounted as a seal
An Arundel gem (Cat. Thec. A, No. 68)

710 CAMEO ON A PASTE IN IMITATION OF AN ONYX. A dog, or perhaps a wolf, lying down, seen from above. Cut in a white layer, by perhaps a Roman hand

711 CAMEO ON AN ONYX. An animal like a panther; cut in a tawny upper layer with a mottled black jasper base; the animal is also mottled with spots. Similar setting to 718
An Arundel gem (Cat. Thec. C, No. 22), formerly united to the gem No. 718

712 CAMEO ON MOTTLED JASPER. A panther couchant, seen from above; cut in a brown upper layer mottled with spots, the base being a jasper, reddish and grey. It is mounted in ring. The bezel set with brilliants

713 INTAGLIO ON A FINE ALMANDINE GARNET. A lion seen in front-face and somewhat foreshortened; his paw on the head of a stag. A dog behind the lion is skulking off, baying. The work is remarkably bold.

This garnet, No. 57 in Natter's Catalogue, was one of the Bessborough gems. In his Traité, Natter describes and figures (No. xvii.) a similar but less complex gem—a fragment on amethyst—in Lord Carlisle's Collection

714 INTAGLIO ON A FINE PLASMA. A lion passant, with his foot on
a bull's head. A Roman work, symbolical probably of the
sun

715 INTAGLIO ON A NICOLO. A sleeping lion; a well-modelled
Roman work

716 CAMEO ON A SARDONYX. A very fine cameo of a lion pulling
down a bull. The lion is in a rich brown upper layer in rather
high relief. The bull is rendered in a flat manner in order
to take advantage of a thin white layer; the base is dark.
The stone has been pierced lengthways by a hole, and
another goes through the face of the gem, where a third has
also been begun. The work has all the character of genuine
antiquity

Purchased for 50l. by the third Duke

717 A CAMEO IN BOLD RELIEF, in cat's-eye, representing a lion's
head; the chatoyance of the material giving a remarkable
life to a work which is otherwise tame. It is by a cinque-
cento hand, and is set in a pretty frame formed of golden
loops

718 CAMEO ON SARDONYX. A lion passant, his tail curled under
the hind leg. This spirited work is cut in a rich brown sard
upper layer, with an under layer of white. It is set in a
heavy gold mounting, carefully chiselled on the back in the
seventeenth century, and similar to that of No. 711. The
work is undercut, and like the panther, No. 711, formerly
attached to it: it is probably of sixteenth century workmanship

It was in the Arundel Collection (Cat. Thec. C, No. 22)

719 CAMEO ON A JASPER ONYX. A lion passant, cut in a tawny
brown upper layer, supported by a black base. A delicately
finished work of the last century

720 INTAGLIO ON A SARD. Three eagles standing upon three altars
An Arundel gem (Cat. Thec. A, No. 97)

721 INTAGLIO ON AN ONYX. An eagle standing on an altar. Work of the second century; cut in a white layer with a black base, and set as a seal with enamelled flowers—*temp.* Louis XIII.

An Arundel gem (Cat. Thec. A, No. 71)

723 INTAGLIO ON A CHALCEDONY. A peacock standing on a basket, a raven standing on a cornucopia, and 'a cock between them. A Roman work

An Arundel gem (Cat. Thec. A, No. 94)

724 INTAGLIO ON A NICOLO. Representation in Roman work of a peacock and a cornucopia

An Arundel gem (Cat. Thec. A, No. 96)

725 INTAGLIO ON A NICOLO. A cock with a wreath in his bill. With the word VIGIL written forwards in the exergue

An Arundel gem (Cat. Thec. A, No. 93)

726 INTAGLIO ON A SARD. An owl standing on a branch. A fine work

A Bessborough gem (Cat. No. 93)

727 CAMEO ON AN ONYX. A quail, as if fighting, in a red layer on a white ground

A Bessborough gem (Cat. No. 83)

728 INTAGLIO ON A SIRIAM GARNET. A frog. Fine Roman work

A Bessborough gem (Cat. No. 87)

729 INTAGLIO ON A SARD. A cicada perched on a caducous. A delicately worked Roman gem

730 INTAGLIO ON A GREEN JASPER, with red bands. A scorpion set as a seal

An Arundel gem (Cat. Thec. A, No. 67)

731 INTAGLIO ON A FINE ALMANDINE GARNET, cut *en cabochon.* A very fine Roman gem, representing a spider in its web

One of the Medina gems (Cat. No. 48 M)

732 CAMEO ON SARDONYX. The Œstrus, or horse-fly, most perfectly represented, of the natural size and colour, in a translucent brown layer, supported by a reddish under layer. It is magnificent work of the finest Roman period

A Medina gem (Cat. No. 27 M)

733 CAMEO ON AN ONYX. A four-winged scarab of Romano-Egyptian work. Cut in a pale brownish layer on a white base

734 INTAGLIO ON A FINE BLUE CONVEX AQUAMARINE. A Hippocampus. Beautiful antique work, possibly cut by a Greek hand

735 CAMEO ON AN ONYX. A Hippocampus cut in a whitish layer with a black base ; in its original gold setting. The work is certainly antique. Mounted in antique gold setting, with loop

A Bessborough gem (Cat. No. ?0)

736 CAMEO ON AN ONYX. A Gryphon in a white layer with a brownish base. It is nice Roman work

A Bessborough gem (Cat. No. 82)

737 CAMEO ON AN ONYX. A nondescript animal, the face and different parts being rendered in differently coloured layers of the stone. It is a conceit of the early Renaissance period

738 INTAGLIO ON AN ONYX. Capricorn and rudder. The signet probably of a sailor

An Arundel gem (Cat. Thec. A, No. 100)

739 INTAGLIO ON A BANDED AGATE. A dolphin and rudder

An Arundel gem (Cat. Thec. No. 101)

FINIS.

London : Printed by WILLIAM CLOWES AND SONS, Limited, Stamford Street and Charing Cross.